RESTLESS PILGRIM

The Spiritual Journey of Bob Dylan

RESTLESS PILGRIM

The Spiritual Journey of Bob Dylan

By Scott M. Marshall
With Marcia Ford

Restless Pilgrim: The Spiritual Journey of Bob Dylan
Published by Relevant Books
A division of Relevant Media Group, Inc.

www.relevant-books.com
www.relevantmediagroup.com

© 2002 by Relevant Media Group, Inc.

Design by Relevant Solutions
Bobby Jones, Daniel Ariza, Greg Lutze, Raul Justiniano
www.relevant-solutions.com

Library of Congress Control Number: 2002109732
International Standard Book Number: 0-9714576-2-X

For information:
RELEVANT MEDIA GROUP, INC.
POST OFFICE BOX 951127
LAKE MARY, FL 32795
407-333-7152

02 03 04 05 9 8 7 6 5 4 3 2

Printed in the United States of America

This book is dedicated to Eddie Morrison (1949-1999) who spoke those words of life to me—words I could never hear before. I will see you again, brother Ed. And to my wife Amy who has loved me, despite my flaws and failures, in this new and beautiful life.

Scott Marshall, Toccoa, Georgia,

July 2002

Acknowledgements

Introduction

Epilogue

Notes

ACKNOWLEDGMENTS

I'd like to acknowledge all those who helped me out with interviews; and a big thanks to Tony Norman who suggested I do them in the first place. I'd also like to acknowledge three authors who blazed the trail before me, the late John Bauldie, the late Bert Cartwright, and the late Robert Shelton. Their work was a tremendous help. Other folks who have written on and researched Dylan's career also contributed to the life of this book: Karl Erik Andersen, Olof Bjorner, Marty Grossman, Clinton Heylin, Michael Krogsgaard, Bill Pagel, Bill Parr, Stephen Pickering, Mac Ricketts, Laurence Schlesinger, Don Williams, Paul Williams, Ian Woodward, and Larry Yudelson.

Many encouraged me through word and deed: Susan Adams, Sharon Carpenter, Dr. Daniel Evearitt, Mark Joseph, Veronica Keohane, Carol, Alec, and Peach Lauriault (the family through whom I was introduced to Dylan's music), Jonathan Lauer, Steve Michel, Anne Nicolson, Jason Robb, Bob Ryan, Dave Whiting-Smith, and Mark Weber. And many provided assistance, including: Dave Colleran, Christen Cook (whose Lennon book I didn't use), Chris Cooper, B.J. Ellis, Jeff Gaskill, and Katherina Koenig.

For the helpful nudges of inspiration along the way I'd like to thank: Margaret Cox, Ron Fuhrmann, the kids at GBCH, Dave Governor, Regina Havis, Dr. Dennis Hensley, cartooning legend John Lawing, George and Kathy Lebo, George and Hazel Mosteller, Mary Neely, Tom Noon, Richard Parker, Davin Seay, and Dr. Michael Smith.

The folks who publish the Dylan fanzines played an instrumental role. I'd like to especially thank Mick and Laurie McCuistion of *On the Tracks* for their giving me a forum for my interviews and articles; and also Tom Porter (hi Blakely), who gave me that subscription to *On the Tracks* all those years ago; also thanks to Derek and Tracy Barker of *Isis*, and Mike Wyvill and John Wraith of *The Bridge*.

A toast must be raised to the family at Relevant Media Group, particularly Cameron Strang who believed in the book and gave this first-time author a shot; and to Marcia Ford who took a 1,000 page nightmare and performed some major surgery with splendid results. Thanks also to Cara Baker, my editor, for her patience and her insights in helping this book come to pass (and thanks to my sister Amy who edited the book way back in its formative stages).

And finally, a very special thanks to my family: my wife, Amy Marshall; my grandparents, Earl and Dolores Maxon, and the late Walter and Helen Marshall; my parents, Walter and Jean Marshall; Cynthia Brown, the LaFrentzs, the Ragallers, the Roseberrys, the Lecrones, and my extended family. And to all, a good night—hit the light switch.

Scott Marshall, Toccoa, Georgia
July 2002

INTRODUCTION

Back in 1967, an already unpredictable Bob Dylan released his most unusual album to date—*John Wesley Harding*, a spiritually saturated effort that marked his recording comeback after a motorcycle crash eighteen months earlier. His fans—some of whom still wondered if he might be dead—breathed an almost audible sigh of relief when the album came out. Dylan was out on vinyl once again, and all was right with the world.

And the album contained some really good material, including one of his most enduring songs ever, "All Along the Watchtower." Soon enough, though, reviewers and critics began analyzing the biblical thread that ran through the lyrics. True, Dylan had been known to write and perform songs that contained scriptural references, but somehow, this was different. Hearing dozens of allusions to Scripture on a single album—and hearing a Jewish

guy sing "I Dreamed I Saw St. Augustine"—raised more than
a few eyebrows.

What was going on here?

John Cohen, for one, was determined to find out. A folksinger
and a longtime friend of Dylan's, Cohen speculated that perhaps
Dylan had fallen under the literary influence of Franz Kafka's
parables. No, Dylan told him, that wasn't it, adding that the only
parables he was familiar with were those found in the Bible. The
Bible? That's right. Dylan told Cohen he read the Bible often.

"I don't think you're the kind of person who goes to the hotel,
where the Gideons leave a Bible, and you pick it up," Cohen said.

"Well, you never know," Dylan answered. It was a wonderfully
Dylanesque answer, the kind that would come to characterize the
legendary musician in countless interviews for decades to come.
And in one way or another, it's the answer Dylan has been
giving for years to those people who think they've got him all
figured out.

Never was there greater speculation about the enigmatic icon than
after his much-publicized conversion to Christianity in 1979. It's
all over for Dylan, the music industry decreed; he's a right-wing
fundamentalist, and there's no way he can keep his creative edge
in that dull, stifling camp. *Well, you never know.*

Some skeptics in the church weren't convinced that his experience
was authentic, like the distributor to some 2,000 Christian stores

who initially refused to stock Dylan's albums. Meanwhile, others in the church were shouting "Hallelujah!" over the news that this high-profile rebel—the very symbol of an entire generation gone to pot—had renounced his evil ways and joined the ranks of true believers. Just wait till he gets his act together, some said; he'll be a model Christian, the kind we can parade in front of the world to show how good we are at turning an ex-hippie into an exemplary believer. *Well, you never know*.

And then, Dylan was spotted in Jerusalem, participating in the bar mitzvah of one of his sons. The word was out: Bob Dylan had renounced his faith in Jesus and returned to his Jewish roots. After all, what else could his presence at such a holy rite of passage mean? *Well, you never know*.

Finally, for those who still cared enough to be confused about his spiritual life, there was the no-small matter of Dylan's lifestyle. Come on—the man is divorced, he doesn't go to church, he hangs out with all the wrong people. How can he call himself a Christian? *Well, you never know*.

And that's what Dylan has been saying all along. You never know what's going on in another person's interior life unless he chooses to reveal it. You can try to judge by the external signs, but you're likely to be wrong.

Just look at David, the shepherd boy who became the king of Israel. Imagine, if you can, how he'd come across if the only bits of information we had about him were the external facts found in the historical accounts of his life and his reign. He'd still be a national hero, of course, and he'd still be likable despite his obvious failings. But David left far more than mere facts about his life. He left a legacy that maps out his soul's interior journey, a collection of songs that express the cry of his heart. Even people with little knowledge of the Bible know something about the book of Psalms. Through the Psalms, we get to see a different side of David, the very private life of a very public figure.

And so it is with Bob Dylan. Journalists and photographers have at times followed him around and reported his every move, drawing conclusions from what they observed. All too often, though, their powers of observation have been either limited or downright flawed. Some have judged him by what they saw, or worse, what they assumed—ignoring the Psalm-like evidence of Dylan's interior life found in the songs he's written and performed. Others have tried to sift the evidence of his spirituality through a cultural grid, whether that culture be evangelical Christianity or orthodox Judaism or secularism. And they've always come up short.

Bob Dylan refuses to be categorized—or, perhaps better, simply *cannot* be categorized. Those who pigeonholed him early on as a folksinger eventually realized their mistake, since his music clearly extended beyond the confines of that genre. To this day many think of Dylan as a 1960s anti-war protester, even though he has never considered himself to be a pacifist. Also during the sixties, even his most ardent fans—who should have known better— labeled him a hippie, which he also never was. Bob Dylan has always simply been his own man. More accurately, Bob Dylan has always been God's own man, long before he knew it.

Despite the pride America likes to take in being known as a nation of rugged individualists, our society has a difficult time dealing with people who fail to fit into the dominant culture's notion of how they should live their lives. What's even worse, though, is that the dominant *religious* culture has the same problem—often, with devastating eternal consequences. If you don't come to faith in Jesus in a certain way, if you don't look and think and act and worship in a particular manner, well, then, you're probably not a Christian. It's that kind of thinking that has turned many a prospective or new believer away from the church—and away from Jesus, since all too many people see the church and Jesus as one and the same. They see the church's rejection of them as Jesus' rejection of them.

Dylan is among those who do not fit the mold created by the dominant religious culture in America. Bob Dylan knows who he is and where he stands in relation to God, even if some people in the church don't. He's been finding his way spiritually since he was a teenager, largely on his own. There are those within the church who consider the solitary spiritual journey to be a dangerous one, and they can point to any number of shipwrecked lives to support their position. At the same time, though, they fail to make allowances for those who manage to maintain a relationship with God apart from the traditional church, those who actually have the wisdom and common sense and discernment to read the Bible on their own with insight and accuracy. Since Bob Dylan is not exactly known for being superficial or shallow, it's reasonably safe to assume that he brings the same philosophical depth to his reading of the Bible that he exhibits in his lyrics. His profound respect for the Word of God all but guarantees his careful handling of the truth it contains.

Whether Dylan likes it or not—and he clearly does not—he is a prophet for our time. And prophets tend to make people nervous, very nervous. They live on the margins of society, unrestricted by the expectations of others. They disturb the status quo. They challenge us to be better than we are, to think more deeply, to care more passionately, to live more radically. They serve as mirrors that reflect the images of the worst that we are and the best we can possibly hope to be.

Musically, Dylan's voice has been perhaps the most prophetic voice in the last half century. He led the folk genre out of the beatnik coffee houses and onto the airwaves of major pop-rock radio stations. He plugged his band into amplifiers, ignored the subsequent criticism, and paved the way for an entirely new musical style, folk-rock, all the while rejecting the music industry's penchant for attaching labels to musical styles. He was country when country wasn't cool, lending credibility to yet another groundbreaking style, country-rock. He defied recording industry executives by releasing a string of gospel albums. And he continued to create fresh material long after other aging musicians had resorted to recycling their old hits; he beat the odds by releasing one of his best albums ever not long after his sixtieth birthday. But most of all, it was Bob Dylan who showed the world that popular musicians had something significant to say. He gave every future songwriter the license to marry substantial and thoughtful lyrics to a contemporary beat.

Spiritually, Dylan's prophetic role has served primarily as a sign of things to come. Two decades ago, he walked away from the particular brand of evangelicalism that initially captured his attention, and apparently, his departure was amicable. He simply moved on, quietly taking the next step on his spiritual journey, one that led him to explore his Jewish roots. Today, neither the church nor the synagogue knows what to make of him. His personal expression of faith is larger than any limitations others try to place on him.

And that is precisely where many believers find themselves right now, with an expansive view of faith that threatens to disturb the status quo of the church. Once again, Dylan has a head start on the rest of us, this time a twenty-year lead. Even so, as far ahead of the pack as Dylan has always traveled, there's something almost first century about him. It's not hard to imagine Bob Dylan sitting under the teaching of the Master on a Palestinian hillside, listening attentively, questioning respectfully, analyzing thoughtfully. Could it be that this is where Dylan has been getting his insights all along?

Well, you never know.

—**Marcia Ford**

1941-1978

CHAPTER 1

Relentless Seeker

In December of 1997, a visibly uncomfortable Bob Dylan sat in a seat of honor at the Kennedy Center for the Performing Arts in the nation's capital. Flanked by President and Mrs. Clinton and two fellow honorees, actress Lauren Bacall and opera diva Jessye Norman, the tuxedoed troubadour looked like a bewildered street person, cleaned up and placed amid the glitterati of official Washington, D.C., and not quite sure why.

One of five entertainers being honored that night, Dylan appeared to be laboring under what one writer would later call "the sheer weight of being Bob Dylan." Few if any people in entertainment history have achieved such a mythological, legendary status in as short a time as Dylan did—or maintained that status for as long as he has. On this night in Washington, the television cameras caught the image of a man who seemed as if he had stumbled into the wrong building, the wrong room, only to find himself to be the center of attention. He looked intense, puzzled, even nervous; at times, it became difficult to watch the private agony he seemed to be wearing on his face.

Actor Gregory Peck introduced Dylan, talked about his impact on the music world and the culture, and narrated a short video biography of the singer. If Gregory Peck seemed to the audience to be an odd choice to emcee this portion of the evening, Peck apparently didn't think it strange at all. You just can't predict who's going to turn out to be a Dylan fan.

Still giving the impression that he wanted to run and hide, Dylan—who conveyed his appreciation for the tribute despite his discomfort—managed to stay put through the next part of the show, live performances by rocker Bruce Springsteen singing "The Times They Are A-Changin'" and country singer David Ball performing "Don't Think Twice, It's All Right."

And then, just when Dylan looked as if he couldn't possibly take any more, an unexpected, magical moment occurred. As gospel singer Shirley Caesar finished her rendition of his best-known Christian song, "Gotta Serve Somebody," Bob Dylan, the man who had barely cracked a smile all night, suddenly came to life, beaming at his friend with positively joyful enthusiasm. The trans-formation was nothing short of supernatural; the Kennedy Center *honoree* stood to his feet, prompting a standing ovation for *Caesar*, who was then joined on stage by Springsteen and Ball. Right behind Dylan was a woman who was just as caught up in Caesar's performance as he was—his escort for the evening, Beatty Zimmerman, his mother.

Critics have had a field day with Bob Dylan ever since his first album was released in 1962. But his critics would be hard-pressed on this night to try to deny what was there for the world to see—a reluctant but grateful and courteous man who obviously finds joy in life through family, friends, and music. And yes, through gospel music. If Caesar had not been permitted to perform that night, Dylan would have been a no-show.[1]

Critics would also be hard-pressed to deny that Dylan was deserving of a Kennedy Center Honor. As a young man in his twenties, Robert Zimmerman—by then known as Bob Dylan—would write an astonishing number of compelling songs that became the anthems for an entire generation and changed the landscape of popular music. With an intensity that bordered on compulsion, Dylan earned his place in pop music history as the most prolific songwriter of the 1960s. His lifetime output of masterful songs, sung by the masses and recorded by innumerable professionals, is no less remarkable.

Virtually unscathed by garden-variety scandals typical to the rock music world, Dylan nonetheless managed to touch off a monumental furor in 1979 with his fans, his peers in the music industry, and especially his critics in the media. But the focus of this volatile situation had nothing to do with Dylan's music or his personal relationships or his lifestyle. What sent shock waves through the industry, the media, and his fan base was the news that Bob Dylan, the symbol of protest against the Establishment, had placed his faith in Jesus. The Jewish icon of the counterculture was now a born-again Christian; Bob Dylan had come to believe that Jesus was the fulfillment of the messianic prophecies found in the

Hebrew Scriptures, just as the Jewish writers of the New Testament had maintained.

No one, except for the privileged few who were around when Dylan had his encounter with Jesus, seemed to know what to make of this. The initial shock of hearing that Bob Dylan— *Bob Dylan!*—professed to have a personal relationship with Jesus was followed by utter confusion. How could this be? There seemed to be no sane explanation for this bewildering turn of events. Some cynics charged that Dylan had been brainwashed, but that didn't compute. The thought that he, of all people, could be brainwashed was laughable. Others argued that he had simply sold out; the popularity of contemporary Christian music was on the rise, and he had decided to cash in on the booming genre. Even his friend Keith Richards of the Rolling Stones joked that Dylan had become the "prophet of profit."[2] But that accusation didn't make sense either, because Christian music sales were still minuscule compared to secular sales. Most baffling of all, though, was the seeming contradiction between Dylan's Jewish ethnicity and his newfound passion for Jesus. Many in the Jewish community felt that Dylan had betrayed his heritage; others, apparently unaware of the existence of *any* Jewish believers in Jesus, found the whole situation incomprehensible: How could a Jew believe in Jesus?

One thing was certain: No genuine dyed-in-the-wool Dylan fan would soon forget this news from 1979. Some never quite recovered; for many a Dylan fan, it seemed the party was over. Others eventually came around and let Dylan be Dylan, whether they understood him or not. And, oddly enough, a few second-

and third-generation fans aren't even aware of Dylan's encounter with Jesus.

But what about Dylan's spiritual leanings prior to 1979? Before his experience with Jesus there were numerous indications that he was familiar with the teachings of the New Testament; he hadn't exactly been silent about the person of Jesus. Before his twentieth birthday, he had sung Woody Guthrie's "Jesus Christ" and the traditional song "Jesus Met the Woman at the Well." In 1962, Dylan himself wrote "Long Ago, Far Away," a song that opened and concluded with references to the crucifixion. His eponymous debut album released that same year contained the Blind Willie Johnson derivative "In My Time of Dyin'," with its midnight cry of "Jesus gonna make my dyin' bed." In addition, "Fixin' to Die," a very rough derivative of a Bukka White song, included a similar plea: "Tell Jesus to make my dyin' bed."

Also featured on his debut album was "Gospel Plow," adapted from the traditional "Hold On," a song that gospel legend Mahalia Jackson used to sing. In the summer of 1962, Dylan attended a concert put on by the New Orleans native; besides being exposed to the genre that was at the very root of American music, Dylan heard Jackson and other gospel singers present a powerful, personal testimony of faith in Jesus. The closing song on the album, "See That My Grave Is Kept Clean"—based on Blind Lemon Jefferson's 1927 original—was adapted by Dylan to include the declaration, "My heart stopped beatin' and my hands turned cold / Now I believe what the Bible told."

Dylan's preoccupation with weighty spiritual matters was also evident in his 1962 recording of "I'd Hate to Be You on That Dreadful Day," a song that depicts the dilemma of a person who arrives at the pearly gates only to be told that it's too late to make amends for the life he lived on earth. "Shoulda listened when you heard the word down there," Dylan tells the dearly departed through the lyrics, indicating that the songwriter believed his Maker would be waiting on the other side. For those who had denied or ignored God, the song warned that it would be a dreadful day indeed.

Having grown up in a Jewish home and been bar mitzvahed as an adolescent, a young Bob Dylan would have had more than a passing acquaintance with the Hebrew language and Scriptures. Perhaps equally—or even more—influential was the gospel music he heard on the radio late at night, when from his home in Minnesota he could pull in a signal from far-away Shreveport, Louisiana, a thousand miles to the south. That station played rhythm and blues, the music of Bobby "Blue" Bland, Junior Parker, Muddy Waters, and Howlin' Wolf—singers and songwriters who would have a profound effect on Dylan's musical style. But nothing struck a chord in him the way gospel music did.

Dylan still remembers when he was twelve and first heard the legendary gospel group The Staple Singers. "At midnight the gospel stuff would start," he said, referring to the Shreveport station. "I got to be acquainted with the Swan Silvertones and the Dixie Hummingbirds, the Highway QC's and all that. But the Staple Singers came on...and they were so different."[3]

As a twenty-two year old in 1963, Dylan referred to Jesus in his lyrical masterpieces "Masters of War" and "With God on Our Side." The former included an overstatement that had Jesus drawing a line on His forgiveness; the latter asked a question loaded with heavy implications: Did Judas Iscariot have God on his side? You'll have to decide that one for yourself, Dylan wrote. Regardless of the answer, one thing was certain: If the pop genre had a coffin, then as a lyricist Dylan had certainly just driven a few nails into it.

Despite these and other biblical allusions in his early lyrics, on more than one occasion Dylan flatly denied having a personal faith. Claiming to have tried out several different religions, Dylan said he had no religion of his own. He believed that individuals and churches interpreted the Bible to suit their own needs. God is all around us, he said, but people don't respect or recognize Him; after all, look what they did to Jesus when He walked on the earth, he pointed out.[4]

Dylan may not have claimed a personal faith, but his own words indicate that God was very much on his mind, just as the Bible was very much a part of his life. As author John J. Thompson pointed out, "What he said wasn't always literally what he believed. He enjoyed toying with the minds of both his mates [friends] and his adversaries."[5] That "toying" was most evident in the on-screen persona Dylan adopted for his 1965 documentary *Dont Look Back* [sic], in which he spoke exactly the way a true agnostic would.

So obvious was the spiritual content of Dylan's epic album *Highway 61 Revisited*, released in 1965 when the singer was twenty-four, that journalist Michael Corcoran would later describe the lyrics as a translation of the Bible in street terms.[6] *San Francisco Chronicle* jazz critic Ralph Gleason, who initially dismissed Dylan as a lightweight, would eventually label Dylan not only a genius but also a "singing conscience and moral referee."[7]

And in their book tracing the gospel roots of rock, authors Davin Seay and Mary Neely describe *Highway 61 Revisited*—which they consider to be one of the greatest albums in rock history—as Dylan's exercise in "turning over rocks in the rubble at the end of time, prefiguring not just the demise of the sixties but some sort of ultimate extinguishment of hope, love, and body warmth. The stops along *Highway 61 Revisited* are more than scenes from an explicit nightmare. They are the summary executions that Dylan, as judge and jury, has ordered up for every metaphysical criminal he has ever encountered or ever fancied that he has encountered."[8]

It didn't take long before yet another role was assigned to the groundbreaking songwriter—the role of prophet. While Dylan consistently shunned this role, it became increasingly clear that he couldn't escape it. Gifted with extraordinary spiritual and moral insight, Dylan had become the spokesman for an entire disenchanted, disillusioned generation. Whether he liked it or not, he fit the prophetic bill.

Like the prophet Jeremiah, Dylan is a God-driven man, although he would not acknowledge or even fully recognize that until he was nearly forty years old. The singer resembles Jeremiah in a host

of additional ways. Caught up in the political and social turbu-
lence of the times in which they lived, both men were outspoken
critics of the governing authorities. And each recognized the
hypocrisy of some religious leaders, a realization that led both to
embrace a highly personal and private faith in preference to
organized worship as part of a religious community.

Comparisons like that do not sit well with Bob Dylan. He once
told *Playboy* magazine that if he had wanted to send messages to
his generation, he would have hired Western Union. But Dylan
had a much larger platform than Western Union for delivering his
messages, whether those messages were intended or not. Among
young Jews in particular, Dylan stood out as a beacon of hope—
an especially unsettling situation for the former Robert
Zimmerman. With regard to Dylan's relationship with his Jewish
fans, J.J. Goldberg, editor of the Jewish weekly *Forward*, compares
Dylan to another biblical prophet, Jonah, the one who fled from
the mission God had assigned to him. Maybe Dylan had not been
sent by God to help Jewish baby-boomers sort out their faith and
their identity as Jews, but that didn't stop them from looking
to him for just such a miracle. As Goldberg aptly points out,
Dylan was just as confused about his Jewish identity as they were.
He could not and would not be the one to lead them out of the
wilderness of their own confusion.[9]

Whether or not Dylan was willing to assume the mantle of spiritual leadership, one thing is certain: Dylan was a relentless spiritual
seeker. Publicly, Dylan acknowledged only a passing acquaintance
with the Bible in 1965, but his mother painted quite a different
portrait of her son in a 1968 interview with author Toby

Thompson for his book *Positively Main Street*. In between those
two dates, of course, the legendary musician had spent eighteen
months out of the limelight following a motorcycle accident in
1966. The time he spent recuperating at his Woodstock, New
York, home offered him an opportunity to read the Scriptures
more carefully than he ever could have had he been recording and
touring. Describing a house that overflowed with books, Beatty
Zimmerman told Thompson that one book, the Bible, dominated
both Dylan's den and his interest. Resting on an open stand in the
middle of his study, the Bible was the book that formed the focal
point of the singer's attention; Zimmerman's comments depict a
restless inquisitor, frequently going over to the Bible to check
something out.

It was into this Bible-soaked environment that a soul-searching
Noel Paul Stookey—Paul of Peter, Paul, and Mary—arrived to pay
Dylan a visit in 1967. Before leaving, Stookey received a significant piece of advice from his friend: Read the Bible. Stookey had
never even opened a Bible before. But the following year, he
found himself in the middle of an encounter with Jesus that
changed the course of his life. More than ten years before his own
life-changing experience with Jesus, Dylan the prophet was also
functioning as Dylan the evangelist. And all this as the psychedelic
era was in full swing. For Dylan-watchers, this was a mind-bog-
gling, surreal concept.

An insightful John Herdman, author of *Voice Without Restraint*,
singles out one of Dylan's songs from this period as a pivotal
point in his songwriting career. Written in 1967 but never official-
ly released, "Sign on the Cross" refers to the sign that Pontius

Pilate had placed on the cross on which Jesus was crucified, as described in John 19:19: "Jesus of Nazareth, the King of the Jews."

"The underlying motif [of the song] is obviously worry, a nagging and disquieting worry about the cross and what it represents," Herdman writes. "Something is now becoming clearer. Behind Dylan's prophetic utterances of doom directed toward society lies fear, personal fear, fear about his own salvation. Now for the first time, instead of projecting that fear outward in apocalyptic imagery, he begins to examine its source within his own con- sciousness...he suggests, too, in the final verse, that this worry may be a sign of strength rather than of weakness. The song, has, as it is without doubt supposed to have, a disconcerting, unset- tling effect...Dylan is asking, and from a Jewish point of view, the question: Was this man really the Messiah?"[10]

That same year, Dylan released *John Wesley Harding*, with its esti- mated sixty-plus biblical allusions; nearly ten years later, he told *TV Guide's* Neil Hickey that he considered that effort to be the first biblical rock album. In 1968, Jimi Hendrix turned one of its songs, "All Along the Watchtower," into a hit that still gets its share of airplay on the radio; most listeners are probably unaware of the direct connection between the image in the lyrics and the words found in Isaiah 28. But Rolling Stones biographer Stephen Davis was among those who did pick up on the entire album's biblical feel, comparing the songs to "new acoustic psalms."[11]

Dylan may not have had a personal relationship with God around that time, but his monotheistic leanings were evident. The closing song on 1970's *New Morning*, "Father of Night," acknowledges a

God of creation and calls for solemn praise. Just days after the album's release, Dylan gave a copy of *New Morning* to an old friend, former New York deejay Scott Ross, who had recently become a Christian. "Listen to it," he told Ross. "There's a couple of things on there about God."

"And sure enough," remembers Ross, "there were some things in there [about God]. They were pretty clear, so I just kept praying for him."[12]

"I'm not the spokesman for anybody's generation. Far from it. In fact, I want to emphatically deny being the spokesman for our generation. Fame is just having your name known by a lot of strangers. People who are kind or good are the ones who ought to be famous."

—1978

Dylan had been the one to open up the conversation about Ross's new life of faith. Clearly intrigued by his experience, he continued to ask questions about what exactly had happened to Ross, whom he had not seen since 1965. "A lot of our earlier conversations in my pre-Jesus days were so spacey. We got into some weird, esoteric, ozone-level kind of stuff. Who knew what we were saying? We thought we were intelligent and profound and deep, but it was just a lot of gobbledygook," Ross said.

"But there were still things we were reaching for. I think what he was hearing in me was something pretty clear, that I had come to some realization of truth that he was intrigued by. At that point, I don't think he called that truth 'Jesus,' but he was certainly interested. And God certainly came into the conversation, and I was clear that my conversion was to Christ."

In 1970, an Ivy League school apparently thought Dylan was "intelligent and profound and deep." Princeton University awarded Dylan an honorary doctorate degree, citing his music as an "authentic expression of the disturbed and concerned conscience of young America" while commending him for placing a higher priority on his private family life than on the spotlight of publicity.[13]

Two years prior to receiving the award, Dylan's family life had changed significantly. His father, Abraham Zimmerman, had suddenly died in 1968. His death apparently prompted Dylan to visit Israel during the summers of 1969 and 1970. Although he went to great pains to keep a third trip private—one that coincided with his thirtieth birthday in May of 1971—the following advertisement awaited him in the *Jerusalem Post*: "Happy Birthday Bob Dylan, Wherever You Are. Call us if you feel like it. CBS Records, Israel."

On May 22, 1971, two days before his birthday, Dylan and his first wife, Sara, visited Jerusalem's Mount Zion Yeshiva, a well-known training center for Cabalistic theology, which is based on a mystical method of interpreting Scripture. Introduced to Dylan by one of the resident rabbis, some American students asked why

Dylan had historically seemed to avoid focusing on his Jewish roots. "I'm a Jew. It touches my poetry, my life, in ways I can't describe," he said. "Why should I declare something that should be so obvious?"[14]

On the day he turned thirty, Dylan visited the Western Wall—also known as the "Wailing Wall"—in Jerusalem, and a UPI photographer who happened to be shooting pictures of tourists captured his presence there on film. After the photographer realized what he had, the photo was published around the world, further fueling the "Dylan as prophet" image.

The reality, of course, was that Bob Dylan simply wanted to go to Israel—a natural desire for Jews, Christians, and Muslims. The timing of his trips was also understandable, a normal consequence of his desire to connect with his Jewish heritage following his father's death. Then, too, an old friend and associate, Harold Leventhal, had given Dylan a book on Israel and encouraged him to visit the Holy Land, according to Stephen Pickering in *Bob Dylan Approximately*.

When Dylan kicked off his 1974 tour—his first since the bike crash in 1966—the thirty-two year old was at another peak in popularity. He made the cover of *Newsweek* magazine, and millions of ticket requests had been received for his forty-concert tour. Concert promoters reported that more than 7 percent of the U.S. population had applied for the 658,000 available tickets.

Another indication of his popularity at the time was his image on the cover of *People* magazine in late 1975. In the accompanying interview conducted by Jim Jerome, Dylan commented on the mythical stature he had attained, denying that he had consciously pursued it and indicating that it was God who had given it to him. He dismissed as unimportant the expectations others placed on him. "I'm doing God's work. That's all I know," he told Jerome.

The following year, *TV Guide's* Neil Hickey asked Dylan how he imagined God. Dylan laughed and asked why nobody ever asked a fellow singer like Kris Kristofferson the same kinds of questions. Then he gave his answer. "I can see God in a daisy. I can see God at night in the wind and rain," said Dylan. "I see creation just about everywhere. The highest form of song is prayer: King David's, Solomon's, the wailing of a coyote, the rumble of the earth. It must be wonderful to be God."

Claiming that "there's a mystic in all of us," Dylan added, "It's part of our nature. Some of us are shown more than others. Or maybe we're all shown the same things, but some make more use of it." He denied attaching any special significance to his visits to Israel but acknowledged his interest in what exactly makes a person a Jew. "I'm interested in the fact that Jews are Semites, like Babylonians, Hittites, Arabs, Syrians, Ethiopians. But a Jew is different because a lot of people hate Jews. There's something going on here that's hard to explain," he said. Then he meandered into astrological territory, suggesting that his Gemini nature forced him to live in extremes: "I go from one side to the other without staying in either place very long. I'm happy, sad, up, down, in, out, up in the sky, and down in the depths of the earth."[15] To say the least, Bob Dylan's spirituality was enigmatic.

In 1977 and 1978, the two years that preceded his very personal encounter with Jesus, Dylan uncharacteristically talked at length to the media about certain aspects of his personal search. Though they do little to clarify the exact nature of his spirituality, his comments offer a foundation for understanding the swirling spiritual atmosphere that permeated his life just before he embraced Jesus as the Son of the one true God.

One interview in particular seemed to shed a fair amount of light on Dylan's spiritual tendencies. In 1977, just after Dylan had emerged from his divorce from Sara, the singer talked extensively to Ron Rosenbaum of *Playboy*. As the two talked, Dylan mentioned his experiences with L.A. palm-reader Tamara Rand, whom he described as "for real…not a gypsy fortuneteller." Noting the accuracy of her observations, Dylan added, "She'll take a look at your hand and tell you things you feel but don't really understand about where you're heading, what the future looks like. She's a surprisingly hopeful person."

For a season, at least, Dylan apparently placed his faith in Rand. If Rand was indeed dabbling in spiritual activity, she wouldn't have been very popular among the Jewish prophets of old. Those prophets were believed to have had a direct line from Yahweh, the God of Israel, and would have denounced the activities and observations of a palm-reader. Their God would have nothing to do with such soothsaying, and neither would they.

Curiously, later in the same interview, Dylan stated that he didn't believe in astrology, despite his earlier mention of his "Gemini nature" to Neil Hickey. When reminded of that comment, he dismissed it with a reply indicating that he didn't really know why people born under a certain sign have particular characteristics or how relevant any of that is.

It was Rosenbaum, though, who drew out what may be Bob Dylan's most extensive quote about Jesus prior to 1979. "Do you think Christ is an answer?" inquired Rosenbaum. Dylan's response was revealing: "What is it that attracts people to Christ? The fact that it was such a tragedy, is what. Who does Christ become when He lives inside a person? Many people say that Christ lives inside them. Well, what does this mean? I've talked to many people whom Christ lives inside; I haven't met one who would want to trade places with Christ. Not one of His people put himself on the line when it came down to the final hour. What would Christ be in this day and age if He came back? What would He be? What would He be to fulfill His function and purpose? He would have to be a leader, I suppose."

The fact that Rosenbaum's single question elicited so many questions from Dylan certainly indicates he was genuinely seeking spiritual truth. He wanted to know what it was like, or what it meant, to have Jesus living inside. He wanted to know why the followers of Jesus fled when it came down to that final hour before the crucifixion. He wanted to know what Jesus would do if He returned.

In the same interview, Dylan admitted that he had never felt Jewish and didn't consider himself to be either Jewish or non-Jewish. Denying any commitment to a specific creed, he claimed to "believe in all of them and none of them." Not giving up,

Rosenbaum asked Dylan about his "sense of God." "I feel a heart-felt God," said Dylan. "I don't particularly think that God wants me thinking about Him all the time…I remember seeing a *Time* magazine on an airplane a few years back and it had a big cover headline, 'Is God Dead?' Would you think it was a responsible thing to do? What does God think of that? If you were God, how would you like to see that written about yourself? You know, I think the country's gone downhill since that day."[16]

On the one hand, Dylan certainly didn't adhere to the increasingly popular secular-humanist viewpoint, which denied the supernatural, neatly doing away with God. He was even agitated with the atheistic stance, feeling it was irresponsible and had negative consequences for a nation. On the other hand, Dylan didn't seem grounded in any firm belief in an exclusive God as found in the monotheistic faiths of Judaism, Christianity, and Islam.

In retrospect, several Dylan observers later saw how his 1978 album *Street-Legal* provided a host of clues about where the singer's quest for spiritual truth was heading. With its themes of "loss, searching, estrangement and exile," as Robert Shelton writes in *No Direction Home*, the album hints at Dylan's forthcoming conversion even though no one saw it coming. The day after the album's release, in response to a question from Philippe Adler of the French magazine *L'Expresse*—"Do you believe in God?"— Dylan gave the kind of inscrutable reply he's known for: "Let's say, as He shows Himself." He later acknowledged that the source of his music was a "higher power."[17]

In late 1978, the cross of Jesus—or at least a representation of it—
was literally thrown at Dylan's feet during a concert in San Diego,
California. Uncharacteristically—Dylan was not one to pick up
anything thrown on the stage during a performance—the singer
retrieved the small silver cross and kept it. At a concert in Fort
Worth, Texas, a week later, Dylan was wearing a cross on his
neck.[18] That seemingly simple act was anything but simple; for a
Jew, whether secular or religious, to wear the cross of Jesus was
unheard of.

Something strange was clearly afoot: Dylan was on his way to
encountering the man who had been nailed to a cross in
Jerusalem some 2,000 years earlier. Although millions of people
around the world had elevated the singer to a near god-like status,
their idol was simply a man, a man who had spent his life
searching for truth and exposing his search through his lyrics. As
1979 approached, Dylan was grappling with everything he was
learning about Jesus.

1979

CHAPTER 2
Moment of Truth

Dylan's personal quest for truth—now narrowed down to the truth about Jesus—had been undeniably accelerated by the number of people around him who had come to faith in Jesus. Four lead musicians on the Rolling Thunder Revue—a motley assortment of friends assembled by Dylan—became "born-again" Christians within a short time following the tour's last concert in 1976. In addition to those four—T-Bone Burnett, David Mansfield, Roger McGuinn, and Steven Soles—a dozen or so others on the tour eventually became Christians or renewed their commitments to Jesus.[19]

At that time, and largely as a result of the Jesus People movement, "born-again" was the term most widely used to distinguish Christians who had experienced a personal and saving experience with Jesus from church-goers (derisively called "pew-sitters") who lacked a vibrant faith and from secular, cultural Christians, those people who used the term by default, not knowing what else to call themselves.

It didn't take long for the expression to take on a negative connotation, as the born-agains drew increasingly distinctive lines between those who were "saved" and those who were not. Some of the negativity was a not-surprising backlash to the religious fervor these new Christians exhibited, and some of it was well-deserved, as a vocal minority of the zealots became harsh and judgmental toward the "unsaved"—not at all like the Savior they professed to serve.

The term "born again," though, is a biblical one that Jesus Himself used in a conversation with a Pharisee—not what you'd call Jesus' favorite group of people—named Nicodemus. The Pharisees, the high-and-mighty religious leaders of the Jews at that time, were so down on this upstart Jesus that an inquisitive Nicodemus felt forced to visit Him under cover of darkness. You can almost see Nicodemus whispering as he utters these words, which his colleagues would have considered blasphemy: "Rabbi, we know that you have come from God as a teacher; for no one can do these signs that you do unless God is with him."

Jesus responds by telling him that "unless one is born again, he cannot see the kingdom of God." This puzzles Nicodemus: "How can a man be born when he is old?" he asks. "He cannot enter a second time into his mother's womb and be born, can he?" Jesus continues to explain what He means and tells

Nicodemus to "not be amazed that I said to you, 'You must be born again.'" But that admonition doesn't exactly wash with Nicodemus. He asks, "How can these things be?" He can't help but be amazed.

As He often did with others, Jesus turned Nicodemus' attention back to his own words. If God was with Jesus, as Nicodemus had asserted earlier, why was it so hard for him to believe that a person could experience a second birth—not a physical one, but a spiritual birth into the kingdom of God? And then, Jesus utters the words that express the sacrifice God made to illustrate His love for humanity: "For God so loved the world that he gave his one and only Son, that whoever believes in him shall not perish but have everlasting life." That verse— John 3:16—is without a doubt the most familiar verse in the New Testament, and it's found in the context of this conversation with Nicodemus.

Apparently, the words of Jesus went straight to the heart of Nicodemus, who was not only a Pharisee but also a member of the Sanhedrin, the highest Jewish tribunal at the time. Though his immediate response to Jesus is not recorded, after the crucifixion Nicodemus joined another disciple of Jesus, Joseph of Arimathea, who was just as afraid of the Pharisees as Nicodemus had been. The two prepared Jesus' body for burial and laid it in the garden tomb nearby, according to John's account in chapter 19 of his gospel record. It's highly unlikely that such a dangerous act, one that reflected a devotion to the deceased, would be carried out by these two fearful men unless they had placed their faith in Jesus.

So the term "born again" has valid biblical roots, and its derisive use in the 1970s did not and could not negate the reality of the spiritual experience that born-again Christians claimed to have had. Among those new Christians was T-Bone Burnett, a Texas guitarist who has repeatedly tried to correct the assumptions of those Dylan-watchers who thought that either he "converted" the singer or somehow manipulated him into converting to Christianity. No matter what, it's highly unlikely that Bob Dylan could ever be manipulated into doing anything against his exceedingly strong will.

According to Burnett, some time after the Rolling Thunder tour concluded, about ten to fifteen people who had been part of the tour spontaneously began attending church or placing their faith in Jesus, though Burnett is not sure why that happened to so many at the same time. But he did speak to biographer Howard Sounes about a spiritual movement that was gaining steam. "Beginning in 1976, something happened all across the world," said Burnett. "It happened to Bono and The Edge and Larry Mullen [of U2] in Ireland. It happened to Michael Hutchence [of INXS] in Australia, and it happened here in Los Angeles: There was a spiritual movement." Somewhere along the line, someone bought C.S. Lewis' classic book *Mere Christianity*, perhaps the most cogent presentation of the gospel written by a twentieth-century author. That one book eventually made the rounds of the group, and at one time passed from the hands of Burnett's wife, Stephanie, into those of Jenny (Yaffee) Goetz, a longtime girlfriend of David Mansfield.

In 1978, during the course of reading the book—on page forty-two, to be precise—Goetz came to faith in Jesus. "The scales fell off my eyes, and I knew that I knew who Jesus was. C.S. Lewis said that Jesus was either who He claimed to be, or He was a lunatic. But to call Him just a prophet, or a wise man, as many Jewish people do, would be ludicrous. He was either God in the flesh or a raving maniac, because He allowed people to fall on their faces and worship Him."

Goetz later shared the gospel with Diane Scheff, whose husband, Jerry, was off touring with Dylan as his bass player. Mansfield was also on tour at that time, and the two women had ended up spending a lot of time together; before long, Diane Scheff placed her faith in Jesus. Little did the two women know that Mansfield, who had also become a Christian by this time, had been sharing the gospel with Jerry Scheff, and had given him a copy of *Mere Christianity*. The book had clicked with Scheff on a philosophical level, and he began to approach Christianity from that perspective. Meanwhile, his wife had been attending church with Mary Alice Artes, who was reportedly Dylan's girlfriend at the time. Before long, Jerry Scheff accepted Jesus and was baptized in the surf of the Pacific Ocean.[20]

Like Dylan, Goetz was a Jew by heritage, but Judaism had played only a minor role in her family life. Like other "secular" Jews, the Goetz family celebrated the main Jewish holidays—Passover, Rosh Hashanah, and Yom Kippur—but without an active expression of faith in God. "When I began to read the Bible, I noticed that the things we celebrated at Passover were in the same Bible that the Christians read," Goetz said. "Then, as I read the New Testament, I noticed that it was very Jewish. As a Jew, I didn't even believe in God. As a believer in Jesus, I did, and I noticed that the God of the Old Testament was the same as the God of the New Testament." At the same time, she began to realize that Jesus didn't come to start a new religion; He came to bring salvation and forgiveness to His Jewish people. "The fact that many of them didn't recognize Him doesn't nullify who He is," she said, pointing out that in the first few centuries of Christianity, Jewish believers in Jesus were simply seen as belonging to another sect of Judaism.[21]

As Goetz was getting established in her newfound faith, Bob Dylan was apparently engaging in his own personal encounter with Jesus. Artes had either come to faith in Christ or had reaffirmed a previous commitment she had made to Jesus; as with so many details of Dylan's life, the facts are difficult to sort out. In any event, the depth of her commitment apparently had a profound effect on him.

But when did the moment of truth occur? When did it dawn on Dylan that Jesus was the living Son of God and not merely a prophet?

Perhaps that moment occurred shortly after Artes, at Dylan's request, asked someone to come to his house and talk with him about Jesus. Artes and a host of other musicians, some from the Rolling Thunder Revue, were attending a Vineyard church located at the time in Tarzana, California. Now an affiliation of nearly 900 churches known as the Association of

Vineyard Churches, in early 1979 the Tarzana group was one of only three Vineyards in existence. Artes' pastor, Kenn Gulliksen, was the man responsible for founding and naming the first Vineyard.

Despite Dylan-related references to the contrary, the Vineyard was not a rigid fundamentalist "sect." The church and its later umbrella organization has always been one of the evangelical camp's most flexible entities—not with regard to doctrine but with regard to worship style. The free and easy style that characterized the services attracted musicians like a magnet. It's not at all surprising that an independent spirit like Bob Dylan would find his spiritual home in the Vineyard, at least for a while.

Larry Myers was one of the pastors who visited Dylan in his Brentwood, California, home. In Dylan he discovered a seeker whose thirst for answers was seemingly unquenchable. Starting with the book of Genesis, Myers walked Dylan through the Hebrew Scriptures (which as a Christian he would call the Old Testament) and the New Testament, straight through to the final book, Revelation. In what he describes as a quiet, intelligent conversation with a man who was intent on understanding the Bible, Myers tried to clearly convey the historical, orthodox understanding of who Jesus is.

In the early days of 1979, although not certain about who Jesus was, Dylan had a teachable spirit and an open mind. "I was willing to listen about Jesus," he told Robert Hilburn of the *Los Angeles Times* in 1980, when talking about his visit from the two Vineyard pastors, Larry Myers and Paul Emond. "I was kind of skeptical, but I was also open. I certainly wasn't cynical. I asked a lot of questions, questions like, 'What's the Son of God, what's all that mean?' and 'What does it mean—dying for my sins?'"

"There was no attempt to convince, manipulate, or pressure this man into anything," Myers confided to Mac Ricketts of *On the Tracks*. "But in my view, God spoke through His Word, the Bible, to a man who had been seeking for many years. Sometime in the next few days, privately and on his own, Bob accepted Christ and believed that Jesus Christ is indeed the Messiah."

Dylan also admitted to Robert Hilburn of the *Los Angeles Times* that he didn't immediately tell anyone about his salvation experience "because I felt they would say, 'Aw, come on.' Most of the people I know don't believe that Jesus was resurrected, that He is alive. It's like He was just another prophet or some-thing, one of many good people. That's not the way it was any longer for me."

His experience only became public after he awoke early one morning feeling compelled to get dressed and drive to the Vineyard's Bible school in Reseda, California. No doubt his presence created quite a stir; even he said he couldn't believe he had done it.

Artes also attended the Bible classes and volunteered at Centrum, a ministry in Hollywood that reached out to troubled youth, runaways, and drug addicts through emergency housing and a twenty-four-hour counseling telephone hotline. Its founder, Kleg Seth, was not a fan of Dylan's music but was grateful to him for accompanying Mary Alice to the ministry's women's home for dinner one night. That visit meant a lot not only to the young women that the group was ministering to but also to the Centrum staff. In his only private conversation with Dylan, Seth recalls talking about the transforming power of Jesus in delivering addicts through the ministries of Centrum and Teen Challenge.[22]

Dylan also attended the wedding of Centrum staff member Michael Canfield, who had told the singer that he had prayed for his salvation for years. The two became friends, and Dylan, along with Johnny Rivers, also a friend of Canfield's, attended the wedding—not bad for a groom who was a volunteer worker employed by a low-budget ministry.

Rivers—whose hits included "Poor Side of Town, "Summer Rain," and "Secret Agent Man," the theme song for a television spy series—had himself been influenced by Dylan's conversion as well as the conversions of a number of other friends. The appeal of material success had worn thin, and he needed something "real" in his life, as he told *CCM* (Contemporary Christian Music) magazine more than a decade later. Something real, of course, turned out to be Jesus.

Others who knew Dylan at the time remember him for his generosity. He bought a car for one family whose older-model vehicle had broken down as they were attempting to relocate from California to the East Coast, and helped another man launch an automobile restoration business, according to another Centrum staffer, Terry Zeyen. "I did get the impression that it seemed this is the sort of thing that Bob probably does very often—quietly and secretly helping people out in need," Zeyen said.[23]

"I told you 'The Times They Are A-Changin,' and they did. I said the answer was 'Blowin' in the Wind,' and it was. I'm telling you now Jesus is coming back, and He is. And there is no other way of salvation... There's only one way to believe, there's only one Way, the Truth and the Life. It took a long time to figure that out before it did come to me, and I hope it doesn't take you that long."

—1979

Dylan attended another Bible study—also led by Gulliksen and Myers—in the Beverly Hills home of Al Kasha, a songwriter who had won Academy Awards for his musical scores for *The Poseidon Adventure* and *The Towering Inferno,* and had originally met Dylan in the early 1960s at Columbia Studios. Kasha, a Jew who became a believer in Jesus in 1978, recalls the atmosphere of their weekly meetings in early 1979. "Dylan would keep us up until three or four o'clock in the morning asking us all kinds of questions, going from the Old Testament to the New Testament," Kasha said. "He would want to try to see consistencies. He would say, 'Why does Isaiah think differently than Jeremiah but they're all prophetic?'...Dylan's investigative mind was trying to see why one Scripture didn't seem consistent to another, but of course, it was consistent."[24]

Like the Vineyard pastors, Kasha wanted to keep a low profile concerning Dylan's conversion, declining to be interviewed and explaining to members of the media that the leaders regarded coming to Christ as a highly personal matter. "They would ask me if he [Dylan] was still Jewish, and I said, 'Like myself, you don't leave that [your Jewish roots], but he's a Jewish believer,'" Kasha added.

Meanwhile, the music industry had been reeling since the news of Dylan's encounter with Jesus had leaked out. Publicist Paul Wasserman, whose client roster has included the Rolling Stones, U2, and Dylan, recalls those very heady days after Dylan responded to the call of Jesus. "I remember Keith Richards saying, 'And you thought you had problems with me,'" Wasserman said, adding that he was constantly fielding calls from musicians who wanted to know what was going on with Dylan and this experience he supposedly had with Jesus. "Everyone was mystified. I wish I knew [what was going on]. You just kind of were at a loss."[25]

Also at a loss were Dylan's record producers, Barry Beckett and Jerry Wexler. Beckett said he'll never forget the night Jerry Wexler called him, confirming their worst fears: Dylan had, in fact, "gone Christian."[26] They'd heard rumors to that effect for a while, and at first their concern was the criticism they knew

Dylan would face. Wexler was equally concerned about how the public would take to what he accurately predicted, that the lyrics in future Dylan compositions would reflect his newfound faith.

In the spring of 1979, just months after his conversion, Dylan began recording his first Christian album, *Slow Train Coming*, in Sheffield, Alabama, at Muscle Shoals Sound Studios, which Beckett had helped found ten years earlier. Over the years, the studios—seemingly located in the middle of nowhere—managed to attract a host of top recording artists, including Cher, Rod Stewart, Willie Nelson, Linda Ronstadt, Dire Straits, and Lynyrd Skynyrd.

But the recording of *Slow Train* would not be like any other Muscle Shoals had ever witnessed. Full of zeal, Dylan tried to interest Wexler in the New Testament. Wexler responded, "I'm a sixty-two-year-old card-carrying Jewish atheist." According to Wexler, that was the end of the discussion.[27]

But Beckett's production assistant, Dick Cooper, maintains that the biblical banter between Dylan and Wexler wasn't restricted to the brief exchange Wexler describes. During breaks in the recording schedule, Cooper said, the two discussed Scripture. Cooper even has a photograph of Dylan taking notes in which Wexler—hardly a religious man—was discussing specific Bible verses; in another photo, the rest of the crew is going over guitar parts while Dylan and Wexler discuss Scripture in the back of the control room. Talking about the Bible and religion was their leisure activity, but, according to Cooper, neither one could convert the other.[28]

But when he was working, Dylan's focus was riveted to every aspect of his new project. He had an idea in mind for the album cover and communicated this to his art team at Columbia; the artwork he chose, drawn by freelance artist Catherine Kanner—who is also Jewish—was right on target. "There was to be a train, and there was to be a man in the foreground with a pickaxe [symbolizing the cross of Jesus]," Kanner said of the instructions she received. "A normal pickaxe has the handle and then that piece that goes over it; it usually does not have another piece that sticks up. It was made clear to me that it needed to have that piece sticking up so that it would resemble a cross. I knew at that point that that's what he was looking for. It was subtle."[29]

As it turned out, Nick Saxton, who provided the back cover photo for *Slow Train Coming*, was "heavily involved in a secret Bible study" at the time, while Tony Lane, Columbia's art director, was also coming to faith in Jesus.[30]

Back in the studio, Wexler was "knocked out" when he first heard the lyrics Dylan had written, according to Beckett; both men felt the lyrics stood up to the songwriter's usual standards. Beckett was especially taken with "Gotta Serve Somebody": "When I heard those lyrics, I said, 'Oh, my goodness, this is great.' It wasn't your typical, corny Christian-related music, having to do with 'Jesus loves me, this I know,' all that stuff. It had depth."

Many Dylan fans, though, didn't seem to see it that way. They weren't exactly thrilled with the new album, released in August

of 1979, less than eight months after the singer's conversion.
Where Beckett saw depth, many of his fans and critics saw
judgment; to them, the album's lyrics depicted a harsh God
ready to deliver the hammer blow to humanity at any moment.
That may have been an unfair assessment, but it was apparent
that a song like "When He Returns"—ironically, Wexler's
favorite—with its image of God with an iron rod was enough
to cloud the thinking of some of Dylan's fans and keep them
from appreciating the image of a merciful God found elsewhere on the album.

Even so, the reaction to the album appeared to be out of
proportion to its lyrical and musical quality. Why were his fans
giving their idol such a hard time over this? Grateful Dead
lyricist John Perry Barlow, who still thinks the album is "great,"
believes that what people saw was the intolerance of
Christians. "Christians have created a fair amount of animosity
among non-Christians by virtue of their own intolerance, so
that there's a knee-jerk response in a lot of people to any mani-
festation of devout Christianity," Barlow maintains. "I take the
view that the solution to intolerance is certainly not more
intolerance. If you want to do something about intolerance, the
first order of business is to tolerate those that would not tolerate you."[31]

The intolerance his fans exhibited in reaction to the release of
the record was nothing compared to the intolerance that came
after Dylan debuted three of his new songs—"Gotta Serve
Somebody," "I Believe in You" and "When You Gonna Wake
Up?"—on, of all places, the television comedy show *Saturday*

Night Live. Though the audience that night took it well, his critics didn't.

Rabbi Laurence Schlesinger, who has written a number of articles on Bob Dylan, compared the repercussions of that performance to the shock Dylan's followers experienced when he traded his acoustic sound—a hallmark of the folk scene that had regarded him as their spokesman—for an amplified electric sound at the Newport Folk Festival in 1965, where some in the audience tried to boo him off the stage. The rabbi recalled being "completely stunned" at the words Dylan sang and the message he conveyed during his *Saturday Night Live* appearance. [32]

Another long, strange trip with Bob Dylan had just begun.

Dylan took his new songs of faith straight to San Francisco's Warfield Theater for a two-week engagement that didn't exactly win the local media over. After the opening night, Philip Elwood's article in the *San Francisco Examiner*—"Bob Dylan: His Born-Again Show's a Real Drag"—set the stage. "I thought that night was a pretty incomprehensible performance and senseless…Not the band, just the whole theme of the material," Elwood recalled. [33]

Because of all of the hubbub surrounding Dylan's conversion, the other Bay Area newspaper, the *San Francisco Chronicle*, sent Susan Sward to cover the second concert as a news story. As Dylan fans stood in line outside the old vaudeville theater, Sward gauged the atmosphere before the show. What she discovered was a contingent of faithful fans who were willing to overlook Dylan's conversion just for the sheer pleasure of seeing him perform again. But this was *before* the show.

What Sward discovered during and after the show was a different matter. Several fans who ducked out before the end expressed their disappointment that Dylan hadn't played any of his classic songs from the sixties. Despite shouted requests from the audience, Dylan only played his new gospel songs, and that did not sit well with the crowd that night. One visitor from England complained that he had stood in line five hours to buy tickets only to come away with the feeling that he had been to church instead of a concert.

In the *Chronicle's* review of the second night—"Bob Dylan's God-Awful Gospel"—Joel Selvin wrote that although some cat-calls and boos echoed throughout the theater, the audience mostly sat in "stunned silence." Sward claimed Dylan's songs were met with loud applause; Selvin described it as polite applause. Selvin concluded that Dylan's conversion to the "opium of the masses," as Karl Marx described religion, reflected the emptiness of the times and had stopped Dylan from asking the hard questions he had historically asked.

Among the musicians who shared the stage with Dylan during the Warfield run was keyboard player Spooner Oldham, who recalls that the first three nights were something of a mixed bag as far as the audience was concerned, with half the crowd applauding and the other half booing after each song. "After the first three nights the rebels either didn't come back or accepted it," Oldham said. "It calmed down, and everybody seemed to enjoy it more. It was sort of enjoyable even when it was weird, because it was challenging to face that kind of audience. You knew the music and message was nothing but good news, so you couldn't be bothered by that."[34]

The musicians also couldn't be bothered by the placards and protest signs that greeted them as they pulled into the parking lot each day. One sign read "Jesus Loves Your Old Songs, Too," which pretty much summed up the message Larry Myers had tried to convey to Dylan; the singer had disregarded the Vineyard pastor's advice to mix in some old songs with the new. Throughout most Dylan concerts, fans typically shout out the names of the songs they want to hear, but during this series of concerts, the fans were more vocal than ever. And it seemed that most didn't even care *which* old songs he sang; instead of naming individual titles, they simply shouted that they wanted to hear the oldies.

"People were surprised by Bob's religious songs because Bob did not fit the stereotype of a Christian fundamentalist," said lead guitarist Fred Tackett. "Bob Dylan was a whole other world. He represented the intelligent, the literate. He was East Coast hip, but he was completely sincere in everything he sang and said."[35]

And Dylan was not about to change his concert playlist to suit the crowd; he had never done that before, and he was not going to start now that he had a new message to convey. Even the concert promoter tried to get Dylan to play some oldies, to

no avail. "Bill Graham came up and said, 'Please, Bob, just sing
one old song,'" bass player Tim Drummond recalls. "Dylan
wouldn't. And then Bill said, 'Oh, I don't care, I'm going to
retire anyway.' It was a funny scene." But according to
Drummond, the audience was one step short of throwing fruit
at Dylan.[36]

Not only was Dylan playing his new music from *Slow Train
Coming*, he also was playing songs from his forthcoming *Saved*
album—songs that the audience had never heard, not even on
the radio. For Peter Barsotti, a Graham employee, that was part
of the appeal of the concerts. To get to hear Dylan live in concert was one thing, but to hear songs that no one anywhere
had ever heard before was nothing short of sensational. In fact,
the showstopper for Barsotti was a *Saved* tune called "Covenant
Woman," with its high note creating a moment of "magic,
complete magic."

Barsotti may have been blown away by the gospel songs and
the passionate performance, but he was clearly in the minority,
at least for the first few nights. All around him he was hearing
fans complain that they had been gypped, which he felt was
more a reflection of a bias against Christian music than a criticism of the quality of the concerts. Meanwhile, he was thinking, "Hey, is it a good song or not?"

"Take a song like 'In the Garden,' what a powerful song about
Jesus' death and suffering," Barsotti said. "I mean, *wow*. I never
thought I'd hear a religious song in my whole life that would
be anything remotely like that. Then the first reviews came out,
and a lot of them panned it."[37]

According to *Rolling Stone* magazine, some "disgruntled fans" did try to get a refund, but by the third night of the run, the word was out about the content of the playlists, and things started to settle down. Fans knew what to expect, and those who were unhappy with that either tried to sell their tickets or simply did not show up. The audience responded positively and gave Dylan his first standing ovation of the concert series.

So how did Dylan himself take all this controversy? Tim Charles, Dylan's stage sound manager from 1978 to1981, recalls Dylan working very hard, especially that first night, as if he was in the middle of a battle. "There was a war going on between the audience and Bob," Charles said. "Bob liked that. He likes it when it's controversial. He made a really good record, and he was going out there to sell it...He didn't disappoint me. I loved the born-again shows. I thought they were cool; they had energy."[38]

That energy was enhanced by the size of the venue, as Dan Fiala, Dylan's tour manager during the Warfield run, remembers it. After playing huge arenas and coliseums, the singer was once again in front of an audience in a theater. "It was like being in somebody's basement," Fiala said. "It was an incredibly electric show, each and every night."[39] Echoing that opinion was Alex Ross, who considered the San Francisco concerts to at times be just as electrifying as Dylan's live performances in 1966. "But they happened not to fit the story of a generation" Ross wrote in *The New Yorker* in 1999. It was a generation that felt so betrayed by Dylan's conversion that they were beginning to call their one-time idol a traitor.

Ironically, Dylan didn't receive the kind of support from San Francisco-area churches that might have made that kind of backlash a bit easier to take. At Dylan's request, Dave Kelly, the singer's personal assistant from 1979 to 1980, called several religious organizations to see if they would be willing to help out. But unless they could be assured that their support was exclusive, none of the organizations would get involved. Kelly was adamant: They would have to cooperate with other groups. Not one organization he called agreed to those terms.[40]

Such pettiness was discouraging, but the Warfield concerts had a significant impact on legendary rock promoter Bill Graham. Himself a Jew, Graham admitted to being "deeply moved" by Dylan's performances, which he said gained momentum and became stronger each night. Calling the concerts "awesome," Graham added that the event was a "very profound public display of personal convictions."[41]

While Dylan was performing onstage at one of the shows, Graham happened to hear the personal convictions of another fellow Jew, Mitch Glaser, who passed out gospel tracts on behalf of the San Francisco-based ministry Jews for Jesus at the Warfield every night. Early one evening, Glaser was approached by a man who wanted to know more about what he was doing at the Warfield and why. He asked Glaser to sit with him in his Rolls Royce so they could talk. Glaser then realized that the man he was talking with was Bill Graham. For the next two hours, the pair sat and talked about Graham's background and his financial support of Jewish causes. Glaser shared the gospel with him. Finally, Graham told Glaser that Dylan was "pushing this stuff down my throat" and asked how he could get him to stop. "I said, 'Well, that answers my question about his being sincere,'" Glaser recalls. "Graham said, 'He's sincere.' So it's obvious that Dylan was witnessing to him."[42]

Glaser met another concertgoer on the first night at the Warfield, a Jewish man who expressed significant bewilderment at Dylan's songs about Jesus. Later on, Glaser and the man met on a regular basis to talk about Jesus, the Bible, and being Jewish in the midst of all that. Eventually, the man came to believe in Jesus as the Messiah, as a result of what he heard at the Dylan concert.

Glaser's presence at the concert was largely Dylan's own doing. In late October of 1979 a man who claimed to work for Dylan called the offices of Jews for Jesus and asked if Glaser would be willing to hand out tracts during the concerts, which were scheduled to begin a day or so later. Unconvinced that the call really came from someone in the singer's entourage, Glaser decided to put the caller to the test, requesting that eight tickets be left at the will-call window for the ministry. "We went to the theater, and they were there. I couldn't believe it. We walked in and listened to the concert; it was one of the high points of my life," Glaser said. "Then we stayed up the entire night and wrote a tract called 'Times They Are A-Changin.' We presented the gospel through the lyrics of Dylan's songs, but not his Christian songs…I was there every single night. We handed out tracts and witnessed to people."

The tour wound up after two highly eventful weeks and rolled on to the Civic Center in Santa Monica, California, where four concerts were scheduled. There, the crowd was even stranger than usual, according to David Whiting-Smith, who heard people screaming, "Bob Dylan accepted Jesus because he doesn't want to burn in hell!" and saw an assorted audience of "rabbis, green-haired punk-rockers, and grandmothers—not your average crowd, for sure."[43]

Also in the audience was a diverse group of celebrities—Ron Wood of the Rolling Stones, legendary crooner Pat Boone, and Bruce Gary, drummer for the Knack. Their reactions could not have been more varied: Wood became impatient with Dylan's preaching and started shouting at him, just as some of the fans were doing; the born-again Boone became impatient with the fans and wanted to shout at them to listen to the answers Dylan was finally giving to the questions they'd been asking for so many years; and the Jewish Gary was impatient with no one and profoundly affected by the music.[44]

For Harvey Kubernik, a writer for *Melody Maker*, the Santa Monica concert he attended confirmed the honesty and sincerity of Dylan's conversion. "There were times in the Dylan performance when any jerk, including myself, could realize that he wasn't faking," he wrote.

Even so, Kubernik felt some of Dylan's religious "ramblings" seemed forced. In Santa Monica, the singer gave his audience a bit of an education on the origins of Passover; during his next concert, in Tempe, Arizona, Dylan encountered a particularly rowdy crowd that clearly did not want to hear his talk about the "Lamb of God, which taketh away the sins of the world." The shouting and heckling continued throughout the concert.

It had been a rocky year for Dylan fans as well as some of his colleagues. No one quite knew what to expect next. Had Bob Dylan, the larger-than-life icon of the sixties, dug his own grave? Would he be able to rebound from the criticism and disgust his conversion had engendered in some of his followers? And how long would Columbia, his long-time label, put up with his gospel output?

To be sure, there would be consequences to Dylan's expression of his faith. He had once again created a phenomenon that simply had no precedent in the world of rock and roll.

1980-1981

CHAPTER 3
Pressing On

To journalist Leland Rucker, Bob Dylan proved himself to be "the gutsiest performance artist alive" at the beginning of 1980. The singer had not only survived the rockiest year of his career, but he also was showing no sign of giving in to the demands of his detractors or pandering to the wishes of his followers. Rucker, who had just landed his first full-time journalism job three months earlier, attended the first night of Dylan's three-night stand, from January 27 to 29, 1980, at the Uptown Theater in Kansas City, Missouri.

That night, Rucker was blown away by the whole concert, from the backup singers' opening gospel set to Dylan's passion and enthusiasm to the new numbers that would later appear on *Saved*. Meanwhile, down on the front row, three Dylan fans who were employees of a local record store were so disappointed at the religious content of the show that they sold their front-row tickets for the next two nights. Rucker couldn't believe they had seen the same show he had. Despite Dylan's "end-of-the-world babble between songs," Rucker felt he had played with an unusual intensity.

"Here was a guy who did a world tour in 1966 in which his audiences confronted him with ridicule and derision, so much so that his drummer quit in mid-tour, all because of his conviction that the music was good," Rucker said. "More than a decade later, here he was, still willing to challenge his audience, in this case a move that cost him a sizeable portion of that crowd. People didn't know what they were missing."[45]

Meanwhile, Paul Vitello, a colleague of Rucker's at the *Kansas City Times*, managed to coax out of Dylan an unusually visual depiction of his encounter with Jesus. "Let's just say I had a knee-buckling experience," he told the reporter. Dylan went on to talk about the disillusionment with writing and performing he had felt just before his experience with Jesus. "Music wasn't like it used to be. We were filling halls, but I used to walk out on the street afterward and look up in the sky and know there was something else," he said. "A lot of people have died along the way— the Janises [Janis Joplin] and the Jimmys [Jimi Hendrix and Jim Morrison]…People get cynical, or comfortable in their own minds, and that makes you die too, but God has chosen to revive me."

God apparently also chose to revive Dylan's stature in the music industry; in February of 1980, Dylan won a Grammy Award for best male rock vocal performance for "Gotta Serve Somebody," despite all the flak he had taken during the previous year for "going Christian." Less than two months later, on April 19, 1980, a twenty-four track mobile truck recorded Dylan's concert from Toronto, Canada, in support of a live album that never came to pass. During the concert, which was also filmed by CBS, Dylan debuted a new composition—"I Will Love Him"—that included a lyric inspired by the gospel of John: "He came down to His own / His own knew Him not." Another lyric in "I Will Love Him" implied that the Jews' return to the Holy Land was a sign of the beginning of the end—and the coming of Jesus: "He said when the big deal is looming / He will be at the gate / He was talking about the state of Israel in 1948."

The following month, Dylan uttered one of his most inflammatory observations during a concert in Hartford, Connecticut, on May 8, 1980. Between songs, he suddenly segued from the biblical account of Joshua entering Canaan to a commentary on the moral condition of San Francisco, where the gospel tour had opened just six months earlier: "It's kind of a unique town these days. I think it's either one-third or two-thirds of the population that are homosexuals in San Francisco, I've heard it said. Now, I guess they're working up to 100 percent, I don't know. But anyway, it's a growing place for homosexuals, and I read they have homosexual politics, and it's a political party. I don't mean it's going on in somebody's closet, I mean it's political! ...You pray for ungodly vice and you'll get it, ungodly vice and lust! But God's got other things in store for you, in these end days."[46]

No stranger to Dylan concerts, musician and journalist Peter Stone Brown (whose brother Tony played the bass on Dylan's 1975 album, *Blood on the Tracks*), remembers the atmosphere at this show, one he called the weirdest Dylan concert he had ever attended. Fully expecting a gospel-flavored event, Brown was still taken aback when he saw Christians handing out tracts at the entrance to the concert hall—especially since they had what he called a "demonic air" about them, reminding him of Harry Dean Stanton in the film *Wiseblood*. The show itself failed to do anything for Brown; the only song he remembers enjoying was "Ain't Gonna Go to Hell for Anybody."[47]

Dylan's inability to generate any enthusiasm during the concert left Brown unconvinced about the singer's commitment to his newfound faith. "I began to suspect that the whole Christian thing might turn out to be another phase," said Brown, who also found Dylan's "infamous stage raps" that night to be annoying. Even so, Brown admits that he himself might have converted to Christianity if only Dylan had displayed some measure of intensity in his performance.

Dylan's own conversion didn't take Brown by surprise. "I'd sort of been expecting it since *John Wesley Harding*, and certain songs on *The Basement Tapes* also had a spiritual feel to them. What was surprising to me was the right-wing tone of it," he said. A fan of the Pier Paolo Pasolini film *The Gospel According to St. Matthew*, Brown said the radical Jesus that Pasolini portrayed had appealed to him, and he had come to see His compassion and love through that movie. By contrast, Dylan seemed to depict Jesus as unforgiving and placed too much emphasis on the apocalypse.

Prior to Dylan's arrival in Montreal, Canada, for a four-night concert stand in April, *Montreal Gazette* cartoonist "Aislin" (Terry
Mosher) decided to draw a cartoon showing just how far the
Catholic church would be willing to go to solve its problems with
declines in attendance and the number of candidates for the
priesthood. Across his drawing of St. Joseph's Oratory—an
immense Montreal landmark that draws pilgrims from throughout North America and beyond—he placed a banner that read,
"Welcome Bob Dylan." The implication was that the church
would even welcome the likes of Dylan if he could bring people
back into the fold.

**"I didn't mean to deliver a hammer blow.
It might come out that way, but I'm not trying to
kill anybody. You can't put down people who don't believe.
Anybody can have the answer I have. I mean, it's free."**

—1980

To Aislin, it was "just another cartoon on a quiet day"—until he
got a call from a representative of Columbia Records. Dylan, it
seemed, thought the cartoon was hilarious and wanted a copy of
it. Aislin gave Dylan the original in exchange for a signed copy
and tickets to the show. The signed copy, bearing Dylan's inscrip-
tion—"To Aislin, 'The Law was given by Moses but grace & truth
thru Jesus Christ' (John) Love, Bob Dylan"—hangs on his office
wall. People often think it's a joke, but Aislin knows it's the
genuine article.[48]

Dylan didn't include the exact reference, but he did indicate where he took his message from, the Gospel of John. The specific verse, found in John 1:17, reads as follows: "For the law was given through Moses; grace and truth came through Jesus Christ." In quoting this particular verse, Dylan was linking and acknowledging the legitimacy of both the old Jewish covenant, the one God made with His people in Egypt, and the new Christian covenant, the one He made centuries later at the foot of the cross.

The promise of a new covenant is actually foretold in the Old Testament—the Hebrew Scriptures—in Jeremiah 31:31: "Behold, the days come, saith the Lord, that I will make a new covenant with the house of Israel, and with the house of Judah" (KJV). It was that verse that Dylan chose to have printed on the album sleeve for *Saved*; to him, and to many other Jewish believers in Jesus, the verse signified the fulfillment of their Jewishness in the new covenant—salvation through Jesus—that God made with the house of Israel. Today, many Messianic Jews prefer to be called "completed" Jews for the same reason.

Karen Hughes, a writer for *The Dominion*, Wellington, New Zealand's daily newspaper, was the first person to interview Dylan at length after his experience with Jesus. In May 1980, a couple of weeks after the Hartford concerts, Dylan talked with her in a disarming way about his sense of God's call. "I guess He's always been calling me," he said, specifically noting that it was Jesus who had been calling him—and that it is Jesus who is calling everyone. Afraid that He will force them to do things they don't want to do—or keep them from doing things they would like to do—people ignore the call of God, Dylan explained. "But God's got

His own purpose and time for everything," he said. "He knew when I would respond to His call."

On June 20, 1980, *Saved* was released, carrying with it perhaps the most controversial album cover of Dylan's career. At Dylan's request, Tony Wright painted the original cover, a piece of artwork that depicted a huge bloody hand reaching downward as smaller hands reached up. If the pickaxe of *Slow Train Coming* was the subtle reference to the cross of Jesus, then the entire *Saved* cover was literally the blood and redemption that flowed from it.

To put it mildly, Columbia wasn't too happy with it. According to Wright, the record company "always hated it. *Hated* it…When I finally took everything in, they were so rude, so nasty about Bob Dylan and said how they weren't going to promote this record, another gospel record…I was just astonished to hear these people, high-up people at CBS, talking about this man [with this] kind of attitude. They hated the sleeve, too. It was really depressing."

Why did Dylan want that particular cover? According to Wright, during the time Dylan was recording *Slow Train Coming*, he had experienced a vision of Jesus' hand coming down as other hands reached up to His. At the same time, the entire concept for *Saved* had come together, including all the songs. "What you've drawn here was exactly what I saw," Dylan told Wright.[49]

Eight months after *Saved* was released, *Melody Maker* corroborated Wright's story of a not-so-happy record company. Reportedly, Columbia distributed the record in plain white sleeves to radio stations because the cover was so blatantly pro-Christian. It wasn't just the record company executives who were agitated, though. A number of Dylan-watchers duly fired their respective barbs. In *Bob Dylan Behind the Shades*, biographer Clinton Heylin quipped that *Saved* was "beyond redemption" and thought the album cover to be "garishly arrogant"; only the chosen few, Heylin believed, should bother to invest in Dylan's latest release.

To John Herdman, author of *Voice Without Restraint*, the *Saved* cover was "almost defiantly vulgar, while the title is a starkly self-conscious cliché." Paul Williams called the sleeve "repellent pack-aging," describing it this way in one volume of his *Bob Dylan, Performing Artist* series: "The cover of *Saved*, and the very title of the record, seem carefully chosen to give the finger to any and all of Dylan's 'so-called fans' who haven't already seen the light." *Q* magazine writer John Harris considered the cover artwork to be "rather nauseating" since it seemed to show "God's hand picking out only the 'chosen' ones."[50]

In 1985, the cover was changed to a painting of Dylan and his band playing onstage during one of the gospel tour concerts. The replacement cover was reportedly what the record company origi-nally wanted but failed to get the first time around.

Of course, most of the songs from *Saved* had already been per-formed on previous legs of the gospel tour, starting at the Warfield in November of 1979. Still, many people were flabbergasted by what Dylan was actually communicating. For Joel Selvin, the *San Francisco Chronicle* writer who wrote the "God-Awful Gospel" review, one particular Dylan song stood out: " 'The Blood of the Lamb' [also known as 'Saved'] was the big rocker toward the end of the concert. It shocked me. I'm a Jewish kid, and I was astonished at the symbolism he was using. It seemed to me that the guy had fallen off the face of the earth into some kind of abyss that I didn't understand at all. Buddhism was more familiar to me, growing up in San Francisco and Berkeley, than fundamentalist Christianity. San Francisco is not exactly a stronghold of the First Baptist and all that. [It] was not the place to bring that show."[51]

At one point, Dylan publicist Paul Wasserman was banned from going backstage, with his boss labeling him an "infidel." How did he respond to Dylan with regard to the ban? According to Selvin, the publicist said, "That's ridiculous. You've got to fire me, because I can't do my job," to which Dylan responded, "I can't fire you, Paul; you're the best in the business."

For his part, Wasserman did vaguely remember the exchange. "There's an expression in AA [Alcoholics Anonymous] about practicing contempt prior to investigation," Wasserman said. "There's a lot of old Hebrew in AA, and when he said 'infidel,' I'm sure he meant I have a closed mind, that I practice contempt prior to investigation. I've never been religious, and I just don't like organized religion."

Meanwhile, Wasserman still had to deal with the media, and the media, for the most part, were downright ruthless in their coverage of the "new Dylan." Bluegrass singer Larry Sparks, whose overt song about Jesus—"I Am the Man, Thomas"—Dylan would later cover, was not surprised at the amount of negative publicity Dylan received when he first professed his faith. "Jesus is not a popular name to a lot of people," Sparks said. "Man thinks he's in control of everything, and he's really not. Man likes to do things man's way. It might work for a while, but it's not going to work [forever]. Jesus works forever."[52]

Comparing the new album with its predecessor, the commercially successful *Slow Train Coming*, Gilbert Garcia of the *Phoenix* (Arizona) *New Times* had little positive to say about the appeal of *Saved*: "This time, however, the public wanted nothing to do with Dylan's brand of salvation. The record swiftly bombed and was ignored by rock radio. Dylan, formerly the revered spokesman for a generation, was now widely viewed as a narrow-minded crackpot."

**"Most people think that if God became a man,
He would go up on a mountain and raise His sword and show His
anger and wrath or His love and compassion with one blow.
And that's what people expected the Messiah to be, someone with
similar characteristics, someone to set things straight, and here
comes a Messiah who doesn't measure up to those characteristics
and causes a lot of problems."**

—1981

In November 1980, Dylan returned to the Warfield Theater in San Francisco for another two-week run, but this time, Dylan would be performing his older songs, much to the delight of his fans. And Bill Graham decided that the "Musical Retrospective Tour" would feature a display of Dylan memorabilia at the theater. Through ads in the local papers and elsewhere, Graham solicited exhibit contributions from fans; collectors who had special items of interest to other Dylan fans could make arrangements to have their pieces placed on display. "We ended up with over 300 things on display there, mainly rare posters, rare photos," said Peter Barsotti, Graham's production assistant. "It was just spectacular, beyond spectacular. We had every square inch covered; it was a real labor of love."

After spending a half-hour or so looking at the exhibit with Barsotti, Dylan called the rest of the band out to the lobby to see the display. "It had to be special for him, because it was his own personal archive collected by people he didn't know," Barsotti said. Dylan's enthusiasm was tangible; he kept calling band members over to look at specific items, saying things like "Come here, look at this." The band got a kick out of one item in particular, a poster from Dylan's Berkeley Community Theater concert on February 22, 1964. "Look at this," Dylan said, pointing to the ticket price printed at the bottom of the poster. "You could see Dylan for two-fifty at the Community Theater." For the record, the 1964 concert, attended by enthusiastic Berkeley students, received positive reviews from both Ralph Gleason of the *San Francisco Chronicle* and Richard Farina of *Mademoiselle*. Joan Baez was a surprise guest; the two sang together on "Blowin' in the Wind" and "With God On Our Side." Not bad for $2.50.

"Then they all went back and rehearsed some more, but I was glad I was there to see that; that was kind of sweet," Barsotti said. Barsotti may have found the experience to be sweet, but who knows what the various contributors of this memorabilia might have been thinking about the latest direction their hero had taken. Consider, for example, the owner of one of the most extensive collections that was lent out to the Warfield exhibit: Stephen Pickering, an "extreme Dylanologist," as Barsotti describes him. Pickering wrote several books on Dylan, including his 1975 effort, *Bob Dylan Approximately: A Portrait of the Jewish Poet in Search of God*, a book that saw Dylan's music as related to the ancient Hebrew prophetic tradition—a tradition imbued with Jewish messianic themes. For Pickering, a religious, mystical Jew, the fire was clearly burning within Dylan by the mid-1970s—and like Jeremiah, Dylan could not remain silent. What Pickering was thinking as he attended these Warfield shows in 1980 is anybody's guess, but presumably he was taken aback by what appeared to be Dylan's apparent sudden departure from his Jewish roots.

And Pickering, as well as other Jews, could not have been very happy with the unequivocal response Dylan gave that week to a question posed by Paul Vincent, who interviewed the singer for KMEL-FM radio in San Francisco. "Is Jesus Christ the answer for all of us, in your mind?" Vincent asked. "Yeah, I would say that," Dylan replied. "What we're talking about is the nature of God … in order to go to God, you have to go through Jesus."

The following day, Bob Dylan spoke once again with Robert Hilburn of the *L.A. Times*, a reporter he seems to have trusted time and again to get the story right. Hilburn pointed out that some of his newer songs "seemed only remotely religious." For anyone who was paying attention, Dylan's response would provide an enormous clue to his spiritual inclinations in the future. "They've evolved," Dylan said of his songs. "I've made my statement, and I don't think I could make it any better than in some of those songs. Once I've said what I need to say in a song, that's it. I don't want to repeat myself."

For Dylan, that was it. Jesus was, and is, the answer to the questions he and his generation had been asking for so long. He saw no need to repeat himself by continuing to write gospel songs or continuing to preach from the stage; truth is truth, and it stands forever. But his comments to Hilburn seemed to fall on deaf ears. Within a year or so, rumors would begin circulating that Dylan had renounced Christianity and returned to Judaism.

But before that would happen, Dylan had at least one more musical statement to make about his faith. Throughout the spring of 1981, Dylan and his band checked in and out of Rundown Studios in L.A. to prepare for their upcoming summer tour and to begin recording a lengthy roster of songs, some of which would appear on the next album, *Shot of Love*.

In early summer, Dylan began touring Europe and attracted the usual media attention—and the usual questions about his faith. That summer, though, particularly in an interview with Neil Spencer for *New Musical Express*, Dylan's answers became less direct and more abstract. Spencer's very direct question—"Do you feel the only way to know the Creator is through Christ?"—was met with a rambling response about the sun and the sand and the stars, and seeing the Creator in the desert and man in the cities. Dylan apparently realized he was being unclear and explained that intellectual terms were inadequate to describe an experience that requires spiritual understanding.

Later on in the interview, Dylan emphasized once again—as he had in numerous interviews and private conversations since 1979—that he saw no incompatibility between his heritage as a

Jew and his belief in Jesus as the Messiah. The Messiah who came, he said, was not what people expected, and they rejected Him.

Three weeks after that interview on August 12, *Shot of Love* was released. One song in particular, "Property of Jesus," ensured that the album would be labeled the third in Dylan's "religious trilogy." Its refrain cut to the core in typical Dylan fashion: Those who were not the property of Jesus looked on in resentment at those who were. But of course, as Dylan sarcastically sang, they had something that followers of Jesus did not have—hearts of stone. Add to that two other songs—"Every Grain of Sand" and "Dead Man, Dead Man," with their highly spiritual content—and the "gospel" label was destined to stick to *Shot of Love*.

Printed on the inside of the record sleeve was the verse found in Matthew 11:25: "At that time Jesus said, 'I praise you, Father, Lord of heaven and earth, because you have hidden these things from the wise and learned, and revealed them to little children.'" This marked the second time in Dylan's career that a Scripture passage appeared on one of his albums—the first being Jeremiah 31:31 on his previous album, *Saved*.

In mid-October, the North American leg of the 1981 tour began in Milwaukee, Wisconsin, and wound its way through the eastern half of the U.S. and Canada. On November 21, the tour ended in Lakeland, Florida, where Dylan treated the crowd to a twenty-eight song performance, including the concert debut of the closing song on *Shot of Love*, "Every Grain of Sand." The rousing, six-song encore included "It Ain't Me, Babe" and "Jesus Is the One"—no doubt a difficult combination of messages for some hard-core

Dylan fans to accept. For so long, they had believed *Dylan* was the one. And though they couldn't have known it then, it would be nearly five years before an American audience would have another opportunity to attend a concert in a Dylan tour. The unusually long hiatus was possibly an indication that the tumultuous gospel tours had taken their toll on the singer and his band.

Writing for *The Weekly Standard*, Michael Long later summed up what had erroneously come to be known as Dylan's "Christian phase" in a succinct assessment that would be hard to argue with: "Predictably, the so-called 'serious' rock press was livid and sneering, with *Rolling Stone* (the journal that took its very name from his words) dismissing his new music as 'Jesus-gonna-getcha' tunes...Fans abandoned him in droves. Dylan, however, plowed on...Yet in this period of depressed record sales and critical spitballs, Dylan produced some of the greatest songwriting and recording of his career."[53]

1982-1984

CHAPTER 4
Jewish Roots

Less than four months after Dylan's final show of 1981, which of course had included a number of his overtly Christian songs, the rumor mill was ramping up for some serious output. With no tour scheduled and no album in production, Dylan was for the moment out of the media spotlight. Maybe it was for that very reason that Dylan-watchers felt compelled to drum up a bit of news on their own. Or maybe their version of "news" was simply a case of wishful thinking. They wanted the old Dylan back, and they seemed determined to create a scenario that made possible the resurrection of the idol they had created.

New York magazine was among the first to question—literally—Dylan's continued commitment to Christianity. In an article titled "Dylan Ditching Gospel?" an unidentified source mentioned evidence, which was never adequately explained or substantiated, indicating that over the previous three years the singer had only been "testing" the New Testament and the person of Jesus. The source was satisfied that Dylan had abandoned the test and returned to his Jewish roots.

The irony, to anyone who was paying attention to Dylan's own words during those years, is that he never *left* his Jewish roots. All along, he saw a direct connection between his identity as a Jew and his belief in Jesus as the Messiah. He could not have been more clear about that.

That notion remained incomprehensible to many people, especially Jews. A person was either a Christian or a Jew; no way could anyone be both. So in mid-March when Dylan passed on the opportunity to present the Gospel Song of the Year Award, to be presented by the National Music Publishers' Association in New York, in favor of attending a Jewish ceremony in California, the cry went up: "Aha! We knew it all along! It was only a phase!" The fact that the Jewish ceremony happened to be the bar mitzvah of one of his sons only added to the speculation that he had returned to Judaism. It didn't seem to occur to the rumor-mongers that Dylan's ex-wife, Sara, was Jewish and had continued to bring their children up in the Jewish faith. It also didn't seem to occur to them that Dylan would choose sharing this special rite of passage with his son over the opportunity to hand out a music award.

The day after the *New York* magazine article appeared, *The Washington Post*, one of the world's most widely circulated newspapers, followed up on the story and repeated an ambiguity and an erroneous bit of information from the article, an error that to this day continues to circulate. The "unidentified source" had claimed Dylan had never formally committed to Christianity, despite reports that he had been baptized in Pat Boone's swimming pool.

The ambiguity should be obvious: What on Earth constitutes a "formal commitment" to Christianity? Did the source mean confirmation? Baptism? Joining a church? To even use that phrase is to completely miss the point of Dylan's spiritual experience. The singer had experienced a personal, life-changing encounter with Jesus, whom he recognized as the long-awaited Messiah. He placed his faith in Jesus, acknowledging Him to be the Son of God.

If this "unidentified source" considered baptism to be a formal commitment, though, then Bob Dylan did commit himself to Christianity. Though he has never spoken publicly about it, Dylan was baptized, a fact that pastor Larry Myers confirmed. The *New York* story—and subsequently, *The Washington Post*—had erred in identifying the "reported" location of the baptism. In a *Newsweek* article in 1979, Debby Boone flatly denied that Dylan had been baptized in her father's pool; her father has denied those reports as well, as has Larry Myers. The fact is that the singer was baptized, and the location has never been disclosed.

If either the magazine or the newspaper thought their reports would get a rise out of the singer, they were mistaken. After attracting so much media attention since 1979, Dylan managed to keep an unusually low profile throughout 1982, surfacing only for special occasions, like his March induction into the Songwriters Hall of Fame in New York and an unexpected guest appearance at a June concert in support of nuclear disarmament, in which he was reunited on stage with Joan Baez.

Then, too, it had been a difficult year for Bob Dylan on a personal level. On New Year's Day, his friend Howard Alk committed suicide. A frequent visitor to Dylan's Woodstock home in the late 1960s, Alk, a documentary filmmaker, had been involved in the filming of *Dont Look Back* in 1965 and a never-released documentary of Dylan's 1966 tour called *Eat the Document*. More recently, he had filmed the singer's ill-fated attempt at a full-length movie, *Renaldo and Clara*, in 1978 and had planned to produce a documentary of the 1981 tour.

In July, seven months after Alk's death, Dylan suffered the loss of another friend, Keith Green. Green, one of the pioneers of Christian music, died in the crash of an overloaded twin-engine Cessna near his home in Lindale, Texas. Like Dylan—who was clearly one of his musical influences—Green was a fiercely independent Jewish poet whose lyrics pulled no punches and reflected his well-known, outspoken convictions. To a world offended by such brash concepts, Green spoke of an exclusive truth, the belief that salvation comes through Jesus alone. He grew up with a Jewish background yet read the New Testament, something he called "an odd combination"; when he encountered Jesus, he had no problem seeing himself as a Jewish Christian. In a sense, Green was something of spokesperson for the believers of his generation—a 1970s generation caught up in the turmoil of a corrupt world and yet grappling for love and truth. It's no surprise that he and Dylan shared a kindred spirit, or that Dylan appeared on one of Green's albums, *So You Wanna Go Back to Egypt*, playing harmonica on the song "Pledge My Head to Heaven."

In late December, in his signature quirky style, Dylan surfaced once again—this time outside the gates of Frank Zappa's home. In his shirtsleeves. In freezing weather. Unannounced. Zappa—who had never met Dylan—at first didn't believe it was really Bob Dylan on the intercom, asking to come in and play some of his new songs for him. The video security monitor displayed the image of a man who resembled Dylan, but the former leader of the Mothers of Invention wasn't taking any chances. According to Zappa biographer Michael Gray, Zappa sent someone else to the gate to make sure it was Dylan and not a madman of some sort. Sure enough, it was the legend himself. Zappa invited him in, and Dylan played eleven new songs for him, some of which would later appear on his next release, *Infidels.* As the two men headed for the kitchen to take a break, Zappa's dog started barking at Dylan. "Watch out, my dog doesn't like Christians," Zappa said. Dylan didn't laugh at the remark. "Maybe he wasn't supposed to," said Zappa. Dylan's burgeoning list of critics now seemed to include a dog.

Even by Dylan standards, his spontaneous arrival at Zappa's house was decidedly bizarre. By now, it seemed no one was able to predict what the inscrutable singer would do next.

In a way, it would be difficult to heap too much blame on those who, in early 1983, assumed that Bob Dylan's strange detour into the world of evangelical Christianity was over. That spring, word leaked out that he had taken up with yet another sect. Only this time, the sect was an Orthodox Jewish movement that was—and still is—little known in areas with a comparatively small Jewish population.

Known as the Chabad-Lubavitch movement, the sect places considerable emphasis on love. In fact, the 250-year-old movement traces its origins to the Russian city of Lubavitch, whose name means "city of brotherly love." The Hebrew word "chabad" is an acronym composed of three words meaning wisdom, comprehension, and knowledge. By linking the two terms, the Lubavitchers— as its adherents are known—intended to show their commitment to responsible and compassionate living.

It's not surprising that if Dylan were to be drawn to any branch of Judaism, he would find the Lubavitchers to be the most attractive. How he came into contact with the Lubavitch movement is not clear, but in the spring of 1983 Dylan began his studies at the Lubavitch center in Brooklyn, New York. Manis Friedman, a Minneapolis-based rabbi who was in Brooklyn at the time, had the most contact with Dylan. Much of the Judaism teaching he received came through Friedman, said Kasriel Kastel, a rabbi at the Lubavitch center.[54]

According to Dave Kelly, Dylan's personal assistant from 1979 to 1980, some of Dylan's friends and family members had been asking him to submit to the authority of a rabbi.[55] It's unlikely that an independent type like Dylan would have given in to their request and begin an intensive study of Judaism unless he wanted to; Dylan was not known for appeasing anyone who placed pressure on him.

And all along, Dylan had maintained friendly relationships with a number of rabbis, even after he embraced Jesus; Paul Wasserman recalls frequent occasions when Dylan spent time with rabbis.

One time in particular stands out in his memory. "A rabbi was at the show and came backstage," Wasserman said. "He was welcomed; no one said, 'Keep him out' or anything like that. We were all joking [saying], 'Thank God, a Jew.'"

What's more, Dylan had continued to study the Torah. Some people found this surprising, not to mention bewildering. Dylan's openness to both his Jewish heritage and Jewish leaders who didn't believe in the divinity of Jesus baffled most Jews and even some Christians. But not his Messianic Jewish friend Al Kasha—Kasha himself occasionally attended a Hasidic synagogue to absorb the teachings of the intellectual rabbis the movement attracts, yet he maintained his faith in Jesus as the Messiah.

According to Wasserman, Dylan "would talk to anybody, and he'd have an open mind." A group of "very religious Jews" often hung around the Dylan entourage. "They would come in and visit, and then Dylan would also study the Torah with them, which made it very confusing." It may have been confusing to Wasserman, but as a believer in Jesus, Dylan would undoubtedly be interested in studying the Bible as a whole, including what is known as the Torah—the first five books of the Bible (Genesis, Exodus, Leviticus, Numbers, and Deuteronomy), which are commonly attributed to Moses.

In any event, Dylan's meetings with the Lubavitchers came at their request, according to Paul Emond, the Vineyard pastor who accompanied Larry Myers to Dylan's home for their initial meeting in early 1979. "[Dylan] is one of those fortunate ones who realized that Judaism and Christianity can work very well together,

because Christ is Yeshua ha' Meshiah [Jesus the Messiah]," Emond
said. "He doesn't have any problems putting on a yarmulke and
going to a bar mitzvah. And he recognizes that maybe those people themselves will recognize who Yeshua ha' Meshiah is one of
these days."

The Lubavitchers, though, apparently didn't see it that way.
Describing Dylan as a "confused Jew," Rabbi Kastel gave this
assessment: "[Dylan's] been going in and out of a lot of things,
trying to find himself, and we've just been making ourselves available...We feel he's coming back [to Judaism]." Not surprisingly,
Emond disagreed with that observation; Jews who come to faith
in Jesus as the Messiah are not seen as confused but as traitorous,
he believes. "When one of their important figures is 'led astray,'
they're going to do everything they can to get him back again,"
Emond said.

**"The mighty King David was an outlaw before he was king, you
know. He had to hide in caves and get his meals
at back doors. The wonderful King Saul had a warrant out on
him—a 'no-knock' search warrant. They wanted to
cut his head off. John the Baptist could tell you more about it.
Roots, man—we're talking about Jewish roots,
you want to know more?"**

—1983

Unlike other Hasidics—who tend to separate themselves from non-Hasidics—Lubavitchers open their doors to spiritual seekers and have no problem relating to non-observant Jews. One of their primary goals is education, and many of their programs are designed to "make things easier for Jews to be able to become more observant and know what they believe," Rabbi Kastel said. In that respect, "Bob Dylan was just as good a candidate as anybody else." He denied his group was taking advantage of Dylan: "We don't want anyone to feel that [Dylan] is being used in any way, which he's very sensitive to. So we're keeping this very, very low key."

Once Emond and Kastel's comments became public in an article in *Christianity Today*, the situation became anything but "low key."[56] Battle lines were seemingly being drawn, and the ensuing publicity may have been what prompted Dylan to avoid attaching himself to any specific spiritual leader or movement in the future. Perhaps the second verse of Dylan's 1962 song, "Mixed-Up Confusion," best summarizes the situation: "Well, there's too many people / And they're all too hard to please."[57]

It didn't help matters when Dylan was spied at the Western Wall in Jerusalem—and once again, photographed by a freelancer who sold the shot to the Associated Press. To top it off, it was soon discovered that the singer was in Israel to attend the bar mitzvah of another one of his sons. A bar mitzvah in Jerusalem could only mean one thing, the Dylan-watchers decided—this was a final indication that he had returned to Judaism. Mitch Glaser, formerly of Jews for Jesus and now the president of Chosen People Ministries, refutes that conclusion; not only would it be normal for Dylan to attend the ceremony, he said, but also it is customary among some Messianic Jews to have a bar or bat mitzvah for their children.

Biographer Howard Sounes, citing "an impeccable, confidential source," said Dylan flew to Jerusalem to join his mother and his son Jesse, who were vacationing there. "They discovered a bar mitzvah could be conducted quickly and easily at the Wailing Wall, and Bob simply flew in to play his part. He still believed Jesus Christ was the Messiah, and kept a broadly Christian outlook."[58]

"As to the Messiah belief," said Sounes in 2001, "is it not evident in Dylan's interviews and song lyrics of recent years [since *Shot of Love* in 1981] that he still believes Jesus Christ is the Messiah? Also, musicians and backing singers who have worked with Dylan in recent years tell me they prayed with Dylan before each show. These were Christian prayers."[59]

In the summertime of 1983, Dylan began recording sessions for *Infidels*, which proved to be far from a secular album, as some reviewers and journalists described it.

One of the best-known songs on the album, "Jokerman," suggests the tension between the faithful and the faithless. Its first line speaks of life—an act of obedience to Ecclesiastes 11:1 ("cast your bread upon the waters"). Its second line symbolizes an utter lack of life—an idol looking through eyes that obviously can't see, inside a man-made iron head that obviously can't think. Idolatry, according to Scripture, is a road that leads to death. Obedience to God, on the other hand, is the path to life.

In "Jokerman," Jesus looms large as the likely inspiration for at least some of the lyrics. We hear of the one who rose up—a permanent "goodbye" at death wasn't necessary. Yet a huge chasm exists between those who believe and those who don't. The song also refers to Sodom and Gomorrah, instantly invoking the biblical account of the perils of unbelief and disobedience. Obedient or not, the sick and the lame are not excluded from the shadowy world of "Jokerman." Opposing forces seek them out—life in the preacherman, death in the rifleman.

"License to Kill" speaks of an afraid and confused man who is also destined for destruction, his brain skillfully mismanaged by his handlers. His resulting walk through life is one of merely sight and no faith. Since his "managers" fail to impart any faith, there is a resulting lack of truth. His eyes serve as his only compass, but they just tell him lies. Like self-contained Narcissus who worshipped at the altar of a stagnant pool and wound up drowning, a similar fate is presumably doled out to the man in "License to Kill."

Even the seemingly innocuous song "Sweetheart Like You" has some hard-core spiritual implications. Clearly citing the words of Jesus, Dylan refers to a "father's house with many mansions" (John 14:2 KJV). Each mansion having a fireproof floor may easily be interpreted as a distinct separation between those in heaven and those in hell. The apparent implication being that those who smile while hissing behind the backs of the faithful are the same people whose fate rests on the other side of the fireproof floor.

One of the outtakes from *Infidels*, "Lord Protect My Child," reveals a deeply touching song presumably written for one or all of Dylan's children. He looks forward to the time when God and man will be ultimately reconciled. But until then, in a post-Garden of Eden world that has been "raped and defiled," Dylan repeatedly calls upon the Lord for protection of his child.

One song from *Infidels* leaves little room for ambiguity—"Man of Peace," a song that affirms Dylan's continuing belief in the literal existence of the spiritual being, Satan, the master of disguise and deceit. Satan, or the devil, is in the end the infidel of infidels, the leader of those who resist Christ. However, their rebellion isn't always apparent and may often be cleverly disguised as truth. The apostle Paul referred to this lot: "For such men are false apostles, deceitful workmen, masquerading as apostles of Christ. And no wonder, for Satan himself masquerades as an angel of light. It is not surprising, then, if his servants masquerade as servants of righteousness. Their end will be what their actions deserve" (2 Corinthians 11:13-15).

———————————————

"I believe that ever since Adam and Eve got thrown out of the garden, that the whole nature of the planet has been heading in one direction—towards apocalypse. It's all there in the Book of Revelation, but it's difficult talking about these things to most people because most people don't know what you're talking about, or don't want to listen."

———————————————

—1984

Infidels was released on November 1, 1983. A photograph on the inner sleeve of the album shows Dylan kneeling down and holding a stone on top of the Mount of Olives with the ancient city of Jerusalem looming in the background. The Mount of Olives, as a geographical location, isn't exactly foreign to the Christian story.

According to Luke, before Judas Iscariot arrived and Jesus was arrested in the garden, we hear this: "Jesus went out as usual to the Mount of Olives, and his disciples followed him. On reaching the place, he said to them, 'Pray that you will not fall into temptation.' He withdrew about a stone's throw beyond them, knelt down and prayed, 'Father, if you are willing, take this cup from me; yet not my will, but yours be done" (Luke 22:39-42). The "cup" Jesus refers to is the upcoming crucifixion.

In March 1984, Dylan agreed to appear on comedian David Letterman's national television show, marking his first announced public performance since the 1981 tour. Anyone who expected a rusty outing after such a long break was proven wrong, as Dylan and his back up band, Plugz, delivered a set brimming with energy; among Dylan aficionados, the three-song performance was promptly assigned to greatness. The evening's set began with a Sonny Boy Williamson original, "Don't Start Me To Talkin'," followed by the public debut of two songs from *Infidels*, "License to Kill" and "Jokerman."

As the summer Olympic Games in Los Angeles, California, approached, an interesting situation brewed behind the scenes. *Christianity Today* reported that Dylan had been asked to participate in an Olympics evangelistic outreach—this, at a time when

so many people assumed that the singer had renounced
Christianity and returned to Judaism. The invitation came from
Dylan's friend and former pastor Paul Emond, who was serving as
entertainment chairman for the Olympics Outreach Working
Committee. If Dylan had indeed abandoned Christianity, Dylan
had "a thousand opportunities" to make that clear to Emond. But
he didn't, and according to Emond, he did consider taking him
up on the invitation. For whatever reason, Dylan did not participate in the outreach.

Within a few months of the *Christianity Today* article, Dylan was
sitting in a Greek café in New York City chatting with *Rolling Stone*
reporter Kurt Loder. During the course of the interview, Dylan
asserted that he was a "literal believer" in the Bible and that he
believed the Old and New Testaments to be equally valid.

After asking if he belonged to any church or synagogue ("not really," said Dylan) and finding out that he believed that the end of
the world was at least another 200 years away, Loder wanted still
more theological meat. Would Dylan ever tell an Orthodox Jew to
check out Christianity? Dylan made it clear that he would—but
only if the person asked him about it. "I'm more about playing
music, you know?" he said.

Clearly, this contrasted with what Dylan felt like he had to do
through his stage raps in 1979 and 1980. The subsequent tour of
1984 reflected more of a musical approach than a theologically
driven one. But his audiences still heard about Jesus in "When
You Gonna Wake Up?" and "Every Grain of Sand."

And while Dylan told Robert Hilburn of the *Los Angeles Times* that his days of preaching from the stage might be over, he remained unrepentant about the gospel shows: "I don't particularly regret telling people how to get their souls saved…Whoever was supposed to pick it up, picked it up."

On May 28, 1984, in Verona, Italy, Dylan began his first tour in over two and a half years, the longest touring hiatus since resuming a life on the road in 1974. However, the tour was limited to twenty-seven European dates—a wonderful limitation for Dylan fans if you happened to reside in Europe. Historically speaking, this marked the only tour year in Dylan's career when he failed to play in his home country. Fans in the U.S. would have to wait another two years before his road show hit American soil.

On five occasions, Joan Baez would also share opening "honors," an experience that, after reading her autobiography, certainly failed to meet her expectations of a Dylan/Baez event. Baez had recently written "Children of the '80s," a song inspired by her younger fans that included this bit of apathy: "We don't care if Dylan's gone to Jesus / Jimi Hendrix is playing on." When asked by Kurt Loder of *Rolling Stone* if Dylan had mentioned anything about his "current religious posture" at their reunion in 1982, Baez sounded another apathetic note. "He didn't bring it up, and I'm not interested in hearing about it."

Baez may not have been the only one feeling demoralized after their short-lived joint tour; some of Dylan's Christian fan base may have experienced similar feelings when it became clear that the tours of 1979–1981 wouldn't be repeated. Dylan's 1984 tour saw a return to a wide variety of songs: His catalog was being mined, and the previous format of "gospel songs only" or "gospel song chunk" was gone.

Even so, Dylan did perform some of his gospel songs, including "Every Grain of Sand" at twenty-six of the twenty-seven concerts. Its opening line confession, combined with a lyric lifted from the words of Jesus, somehow failed to convince the masses that Dylan still belonged to the man from Galilee. In addition, he played "When You Gonna Wake Up?" on a number of occasions, as well as "Man of Peace."

However, the overwhelming majority of songs Dylan chose to sing on his 1984 tour were the time-honored crowd favorites from the 1960s. Dylan obviously felt comfortable singing his older songs. Was this a case of individual Christian liberty? It seems that Dylan thought so; back in 1980, he had come to the realization his older songs weren't "anti-God," and they returned to the playlist.

Bryan Styble of *CCM Magazine* made this observation about his mix of gospel and secular songs: "Anyone as artistically inquisitive as Dylan will certainly evolve further spiritually…Dylan is unlikely to discard the faith that has given him so much fulfillment over the past few years. He has stated his beliefs quite clearly for all who care to hear with an unbiased ear, and Christians can rejoice that Bob Dylan is one of their brothers."

Whatever Dylan's 1984 concert choices were, and whatever interpretations ensued, Dylan resumed exercising his gift—making music and singing for anyone who cared to listen. Many relieved souls no doubt celebrated the set list variety.

1985-1989

CHAPTER 5
Words of Truth

In the middle of a series of recording sessions that would spawn a number of entries on his 1985 release, *Empire Burlesque*, Dylan stepped away for a few hours to join forty other singers for the recording of "We Are the World," the Michael Jackson and Lionel Richie composition that would serve as the theme song for the upcoming Live Aid charity concert. The massive project, produced by Quincy Jones, drew a wide range of performers, including Harry Belafonte, Ray Charles, Waylon Jennings, Cyndi Lauper, Bruce Springsteen, Tina Turner, and Paul Simon. And it also drew attention to the cause of alleviating world hunger. But attention, it seems, is about all Dylan expected the poor of the world to get from the effort.

"It's almost like guilt money: Some guy halfway around the world is starving so, OK, put ten bucks in the barrel, then you can feel you don't have to have a guilty conscience about it," he later told Mikal Gilmore for the *L.A. Herald Examiner*. "Obviously, on some level it does help, but as far as any sweeping movement to destroy hunger and poverty, I don't see that happening." The sixties icon had apparently witnessed the futility of expecting mass movements to do much good, though he willingly continued to lend his support to a number of charitable causes.

Dylan also spoke with Bill Flanagan, who was conducting interviews for his book, *Written in My Soul: Rock's Greatest Songwriters*. Referring to Dylan's "I Dreamed I Saw St. Augustine," Flanagan pointed out that Dylan was one of those rare artists who has the courage to acknowledge that every person is capable of being a villain.

"Well, I don't mind taking that position, because that's just a true statement," replied Dylan. "We're all sinners. People seem to think that because their sins are different from other people's sins, they're not sinners. People don't like to think of themselves as sinners. It makes them feel uncomfortable. 'What do you mean a sinner?' It puts them at a disadvantage in their mind. Most people walking around have this strange conception that they're born good, that they're really good people—but the *world* has just made a mess of their lives…But it's not hard for me to identify with anybody who's on the wrong side. We're all on the wrong side, really."

Dylan also pointed out to Flanagan that a biblical thread runs through all of American culture, "whether people know it or not." The Bible was the founding book of the founding fathers, said

Dylan, and its influence, no matter where in the country a person goes, is impossible to avoid. "Those ideas were true then, and they're true now," he insisted. But what did all this have to do with songwriting? "They're scriptural, spiritual laws…if you're familiar with those concepts you'll probably find enough of them in my stuff. Because I always get back to that," he said.

Flanagan wasn't the only one in the spring of 1985 to hear about Dylan's longstanding relationship with the Good Book. In search of feedback after recording some of the songs that would become *Empire Burlesque*, Dylan visited an old pal whose legend was securely established in the 1950s and 1960s—poet Allen Ginsberg. Raymond Foye, cofounder of Hanuman Books, was at Ginsberg's apartment at the time. "At one point Ginsberg thought he detected a quasi-religious overtone," Foye said. "'Aha!' he said sarcastically, 'I see you still have the judgment of Jehovah hanging over our heads!' 'You just don't know God,' Dylan replied, twice as sarcastic. 'Yeah, I never met the guy,' countered Ginsberg."

Ginsberg himself recounted this exchange for interviewer Wes Stace. "There was a great deal of judgmental Jehovaic or 'Nobodaddy'—'nobody daddy up in heaven'—a figure of judgmental hyper-rationality," recalled Ginsberg. "And he [Dylan] said, 'Allen, do you have a quarrel with God?' and I said, 'I've never met the man' and he said, 'Then you have a quarrel with God.' And I said, 'Well, I didn't start anything!'"

For Ginsberg, a self-professing non-theistic Buddhist, this amounted to Dylan's mistake, a "fixed notion of divinity." The ancient Jews warned against the mistake of naming the name of God, Ginsberg reminded Stace.

However, if Yahweh was anything in the Hebrew Scriptures, He certainly wasn't pliable. When Moses hid his face—amid the holy terror of the burning bush experience—and asked God His name, he was given this fixed-notion-of-divinity response: "I Am who I Am." Moses wondered whether his fellow Israelites would listen to, much less believe, this report. Nearly 1,500 years later, in the middle of a heated discussion with the religious leaders of His day, Jesus had the nerve to say, "Before Abraham was born, I Am!" In making that bold statement, He made Himself equal with Yahweh—Jehovah God—and that required a stoning, which Jesus managed to elude. Whether in twentieth century America or first century Palestine, fixed notions of divinity aren't always popular.

"When I think of mystery, I don't think about myself. I think of the universe, like why does the moon rise when the sun falls? Caterpillars turn into butterflies?"

—1985

Although Ginsberg heard evidence of a judgmental God in the songs of *Empire Burlesque*, another old Dylan friend, Larry "Ratso" Sloman, believed the album contained "none of the finger-pointing polemics that turned off so many Dylan fans during the *Slow Train/Saved* period." But Sloman's interpretation wasn't shared by Nigel Hinton, who thought Dylan had adopted "this unfortunate tendency to crow about the fate of 'non-believers.'" One of the songs from *Empire Burlesque*, "Something's Burning, Baby," expressed the same bitterness, he thought, as did Dylan's master-piece of 1965, "Positively 4th Street," but on a global, apocalyptic scale. Although Hinton considered it to be an excellent song, he still viewed it as unpleasant. He could not get past the sense that he was being addressed by a "doom-laden, holier-than-thou preacher."

Following the release of *Empire Burlesque*, Dylan attended a Leonard Cohen concert in Los Angeles. A few months earlier in Switzerland, Cohen had spoken out about Dylan's *Slow Train Coming*. "Dylan, to my way of thinking, is the Picasso of song," said Cohen. "People came to me when he put out his Christian record and said, 'This guy's finished. He can't speak to us anymore.' I thought those were some of the most beautiful gospel songs that have ever entered the whole landscape of gospel music."[60]

On July 13, 1985, Dylan continued speaking through his music at the Live Aid concert, performing with Ron Wood and Keith Richards of the Rolling Stones just before the grand finale. Although in his introduction actor Jack Nicholson had described Dylan as "transcendent," the ensuing performance from the three musicians has been described as not-so-transcendent. This was due in no small part to a technical problem; the three couldn't hear their monitors, and as Dylan later commented to Robert Hilburn of the *Los Angeles Times*, "We couldn't even hear our own voices, and when you can't hear, you can't play; you don't have any timing." To Clinton Heylin, that was an understatement; the way he saw it, Richards played as if he was appearing "on some other planet that was not as yet receiving this global broadcast."[61]

With Wood and Richards backing him up, Dylan sang "Ballad of Hollis Brown," "When the Ship Comes In," and "Blowin' in the Wind." After the first song he encouraged his audience, estimated at one billion people or 20 percent of the world's population, to also remember the plight of those struggling in the U.S., especially the American farmer. Considering that the concert was a benefit intended to aid famine-stricken Africa, some people thought Dylan was out of line in diverting attention to the U.S. But his comments ultimately inspired Willie Nelson and Neil Young to organize the first Farm Aid concert, which was held just two months after Live Aid. Farm Aid has since become an annual benefit concert prompted by the many letters Dylan said he had received from people whose farms were being repossessed.

Although Dylan performed at Live Aid, Farm Aid, and even a poetry festival in Moscow, he chose not to tour in 1985. And now that he was off the road again, he became downright chatty with the media. Dylan may have felt that the time to preach onstage had passed, but it seemed he decided to preach in the interview arena instead, adding a salty word here and there for emphasis: "The Bible says 'Even a fool, when he keeps his mouth shut, is counted wise,' but it comes from the Bible, so it can be cast off as being too, quote, religious," he told journalist Cameron Crowe for the liner notes to the compilation album *Biograph*. "Make something religious and people don't have to deal with it, they can say it's irrelevant. 'Repent, the Kingdom of God is at hand.'...Tell that to someone, and you become their enemy. There does come a time, though, when you have to face facts, and the truth is true whether you wanna believe it or not; it doesn't need you to make it true...That lie about everybody having their own truth inside of them has done a lot of damage and made people crazy."

Crowe also heard what amounted to Dylan's endorsement for eternity, his pilgrim philosophy in this world, and perhaps a swipe at the abortion industry. "I think that this world is just a passing-through place and that the dead have eyes," said Dylan. "And that even the unborn can see and I don't care who knows it. I don't know, I can go off on tangents…things that got nothing to do with music…God is still the judge and the devil still rules the world, so what's different?" continued Dylan. "No matter how big you think you are, history is gonna roll over you. Sound like a preacher, don't I?"

Dylan's reference to the devil being the "ruler of this world" is drawn directly from the words of Jesus: "Now judgment is upon this world; now the ruler of this world shall be cast out. And I, if I be lifted up from the earth, will draw all men to Myself…I will not speak much more with you, for the ruler of the world is coming, and he has nothing in Me; but that the world may know that I love the Father, and as the Father gave Me commandment, even so I do…and concerning judgment, because the ruler of this world has been judged" (John 12:31-32, 14:30-31, and 16:11 NAS).

The singer emphasized to Crowe that he liked to keep his values "scripturally straight" and preferred to stay a part of "the stuff that don't change."

Dylan also waxed theological in an interview with Scott Cohen for *Spin* magazine. After describing the unusual circumstances surrounding his 1954 bar mitzvah—involving an Orthodox rabbi who suddenly appeared in Hibbing, Minnesota, in the dead of winter and stayed for one year, just long enough for Bobby

Zimmerman to be bar mitzvahed—he proceeded to debunk the self-imposed labels used by both Jews and Christians. Just as Christians separate themselves into Baptist, Assembly of God, Methodist, Calvinist, and the like, he said, so also do Jews separate themselves, into the Orthodox, Conservative, and Reform branches, "as if God calls them that."

Dylan also shared these thoughts with Cohen: "Whenever anybody does something in a big way, it's always rejected at home and accepted someplace else. For instance, that could apply to Buddha. Who was Buddha? An Indian. Who are Buddhists? Chinese, Japanese, Asian people. They make up the big numbers in Buddhism. It's the same way with Jesus being a Jew. Who did He appeal to? He appeals to people who want to get into Heaven in a big way."[62]

In a rather remarkable rant, Dylan even expounded on his idea of the upcoming messianic kingdom: "There will be a run on godliness, just like now there's a run on refrigerators, headphones, and fishing gear. It's going to be a matter of survival. People are going to be running to find out about God, and who are they going to run to? They're gonna run to the Jews, 'cause the Jews wrote the book, and you know what? The Jews ain't gonna know. They're too busy in the fur business and in the pawnshops and in sending their kids to some atheist school. They're too busy doing all that stuff to know. People who believe in the coming of the Messiah live their lives right now as if He was here."[63]

Dylan's barbs directed at "the Jews" invite misinterpretation, but what Dylan appeared to be getting at was the state of contemporary American culture—a secular, materialistic culture that produces "God Is Dead" headlines and the ultimately ironic concept of a "Jewish atheist," the term Jerry Wexler even used to ward off Dylan's preachy ways during the recording of *Slow Train Coming*. Rather than displaying contempt for his heritage and that of his family and many of his friends, Dylan was decrying cultural decay.

In his first television network interview ever, and the only one to date, Dylan chatted with Bob Brown for ABC's *20/20* program, which aired in the fall of 1985. Dylan wasn't at all shy in expressing his personal beliefs before Brown and millions of viewers as he sat in his backyard in Malibu, with the crashing surf of the Pacific Ocean behind him.

When asked how effective he thought "political statements" could be, Dylan not surprisingly returned to his biblical worldview: "People can change things and make a difference…there's a lot of false prophets around though, and that's the trouble. People say they think they know what's right and [they] get people to follow them 'cause they have a certain type of charisma…[so] there are always people willing to take over, you know, [because] people want a leader…and there will be more and more of them [false prophets]." Much of what didn't appear on the show was even more revealing; outtakes show Dylan expressing a clear belief in the resurrection of Jesus and the coming of a messianic kingdom.

1986

After a year filled with interviews, and a few one-off performances, Dylan took to the road in 1986, planting the seeds for what soon would become known as the Never Ending Tour. Although rumors and most accounts in the media had Dylan waving goodbye to Jesus, there were those who paid closer attention and saw an altogether different picture. Anyone who attended Dylan's concerts in Australia that year would have heard Dylan close his set each night with "In the Garden"—and an on-stage rap about the song. One such rap even made it to television, on an HBO special: "This last song now is all about my hero. Everybody's got a hero. Where I come from, there's a lot of heroes. Plenty of them. John Wayne, Clark Gable, Richard Nixon, Ronald Reagan, Michael Jackson, Bruce Springsteen. They're all heroes to some people. Anyway, I don't care nothing about those people [as heroes]. I have my own hero. I'm going to sing about Him right now."

After returning from the tour of Australia and Japan, Dylan granted an interview to Mikal Gilmore for *Rolling Stone* magazine. At one point, the journalist referred to critics who charged that songs like "Slow Train" and "Union Sundown" indicated that Dylan was moving a bit to the right. Dylan's lifelong impatience with labels came through in his reply; as far as he was concerned, there was no right or left, only truth and untruth, honesty and hypocrisy. There's nothing in the Bible about right or left, he continued, adding this telling comment: "I hate to keep beating people over the head with the Bible, but that's the only instrument I know, the only thing that stays true."

Near the end of the 1986 summer tour, the forty-five-year-old singer arrived in Mountain View, California. During a rehearsal sound check at the Shoreline Amphitheater, Dylan, along with his support band, Tom Petty and the Heartbreakers, videotaped a version of Fred Rose's song "Thank God," a song that Hank Williams also recorded.

Oddly enough, the following month, the tape of this gospel song was given to the Lubavitchers—the same Orthodox Jewish community Dylan studied with three years earlier—for the annual Chabad charity telethon. The Dylan version that they used omitted a verse that made a clear reference to Jesus; however, Jesus is certainly implied throughout the rest of the old gospel song.

Even so, Rabbi Schlesinger saw Dylan's appearance at this Chabad telethon, and future Chabad telethons, as an indication that he no longer considered himself a Christian. "From the standpoint of the traditional Jewish law and custom that they [the Lubavitchers] observe, it is almost inconceivable to believe that these Jews, in particular, would actually showcase someone whom they and their audience considered to be an out-and-out 'mumar' [an apostate]," he said.

While Schlesinger and others have viewed Dylan's association with Chabad as reasonable evidence that he no longer maintains his faith in Jesus, it's worth noting that the very concert from which "Thank God" was pulled was the same concert at which Dylan sang "Shot of Love," "Gotta Serve Somebody," and "In the Garden."

Mitch Glaser doesn't see any inherent contradictions. "His support for Chabad is not at all disturbing, because a lot of us support Jewish causes," Glaser said. "It's not like we became Christians and all of a sudden we're no longer Jews. We're very much Jews...But it wouldn't matter to Chabad [if Dylan still believed in Jesus]; that would not keep them from inviting him. They're not like that." In addition to donating the videotape of his "Thank God" performance, Dylan also taped a public service announcement for the Chabad ministry, lending his support for their drug rehabilitation and education programs.

On August 8, 1986, *Knocked Out Loaded*, an album of eight songs that included three covers ("You Wanna Ramble," "They Killed Him," and "Precious Memories") was released. Clocking in at only thirty-five minutes, recorded at different sessions over a two-year period, and not exactly loaded with hits, it quickly became an easy target for critics. "Obviously, I'm not gonna be around forever," Dylan told Gilmore for *Rolling Stone*. "That day's gonna come when there aren't gonna be any more records, and then people won't be able to say, 'Well, this one's not as good as the last one.'"

But the eleven-minute epic from *Knocked Out Loaded*, "Brownsville Girl," was by itself worth the price of admission. As for the three cover songs on the album, some old friends were enlisted for the recording sessions. Al Kooper sat in on keyboards for "They Killed Him," Larry Myers, Dylan's pastor from the Vineyard days, played mandolin on "Precious Memories," and T-Bone Burnett played guitar on "You Wanna Ramble."

1987

A much-hyped Bob Dylan/Grateful Dead tour kicked off in the summer of 1987, on the heels of their twin bill of four stadium concerts the previous summer. During this tour, an unusually large number of songs were reintroduced after long absences, while other songs made their first-ever concert appearances. Dylan would later credit his friend Jerry Garcia with helping him to rediscover his back catalog.

One of the surprising aspects of the tour was the number of Dylan songs from the 1979-1981 period included in the setlists. "Dead Man, Dead Man" includes a biting lyric about those under Satan's control who curse God with their every move, as well as a uniquely Dylanesque image of sin being politicized amid the glamour of bright lights. Other biblically inspired tunes offered up in the summer's sweltering heat included "Gotta Serve Somebody," "Slow Train," and "Heart of Mine." According to Grateful Dead publicist Dennis McNally, the decision to play these particular songs was simply a result of Dylan's suggestion. And two of the seven tracks that would eventually comprise the live album *Dylan & The Dead* were "Slow Train" and "Gotta Serve Somebody."

Robert Hilburn of the *Los Angeles Times* covered Dylan's first-ever concerts in Israel, in Tel Aviv and Jerusalem. His report, following the Tel Aviv show of September 5, 1987, touched on the controversy regarding the Jewish singer's biblical faith—a faith that looked to both testaments and manifested itself through song. Though he surprised the audience of 40,000 by singing "Go Down, Moses," a traditional song about the Israelites finally breaking free from Egyptian oppression, that didn't seem to compensate for his decision to include the Christian song "In the Garden." To some, the mix of songs sent a mixed message about his faith.

The fact that the songs represented a mixed message is due to perhaps history's greatest tragedy, that Jesus has largely been dismissed by Jews though He was Himself a Jew. In typical contrarian fashion, Dylan wasn't one to ignore Jesus. Writing the lyrics to "In the Garden" in 1979—eight years before presenting the song to a restless Tel Aviv audience—appeared to be an attempt to get at the root of the truth, cutting through centuries of evil deeds committed by and falsehoods uttered by professing Christians, and ultimately returning to the original source material, the first-century Gospel accounts. Three of the four accounts were written by Jewish men who became convinced, following the resurrection, that Jesus was the Messiah, the Son of God.

Tom Petty, Dylan's faithful bandleader during the course of the Tel Aviv gig, seemed to concur with Hilburn's assessment that the evening was a disappointing one. But Petty did not believe that was Dylan's fault. "The crowd seemed weird to me...If Bob didn't do exactly what they wanted him to do, they weren't going to get behind him. It was like they weren't going to be satisfied unless he parted the Red Sea for them," Petty told Hilburn. Two nights later in Jerusalem, the crowd—satisfied or not—heard both "Gotta Serve Somebody" and "Slow Train," the latter of which ended prematurely as the sound system short-circuited, ending the concert.

A couple of weeks after his Israeli sojourn, Dylan visited the only synagogue in Finland, included "Gotta Serve Somebody" in his Helsinki concert, and concluded his next concert with "In the Garden." A week later he celebrated Rosh Hashanah, the Jewish New Year, with an Israeli dignitary in Rome. Throughout the tour, the one book he kept next to his journal was the Bible, according to biographer Heylin. To describe Dylan's expression of faith as eclectic would clearly be understated but accurate.

1988

In 1988 Dylan traveled to New York City for his induction into the Rock and Roll Hall of Fame. On the heels of a Bruce Springsteen speech honoring Dylan, the poet from Minnesota took the podium and said hello to Muhammad Ali, who was in the crowd, and acknowledged and thanked Little Richard and Alan Lomax for their help in promoting his career. Later in June, Dylan tipped his hat to one of his boyhood heroes and a rock 'n' roll pioneer—Chuck Berry—by singing "Nadine" in Berry's hometown of St. Louis, Missouri.

Dylan's new album release at the time, *Down in the Groove*, was similar to its predecessor, *Knocked Out Loaded*. Recorded over a longer-than-usual period of time, the release had its share of non-Dylan originals; six of the ten songs were cover versions, which amounted to plenty of ammunition for some of Dylan's critics. "There's no rule that claims that anyone must write their own songs. And I do. I write a lot of songs. But so what, you know?" Dylan lamented to journalist Kathryn Baker. "You can take

another song somebody else has written, and you can make it
yours. I'm not saying I made a definitive version of anything with
this last record, but I liked the songs. Every so often you've
gotta sing songs that're out there. You just have to, just to keep
yourself straight."

Highlights of *Down in the Groove* included "Silvio," a song given to
Dylan by Grateful Dead lyricist Robert Hunter that later became
a Dylan concert staple, impassioned versions of "Shenandoah"
and "Rank Strangers to Me," and an outtake from the 1983 *Infidels*
sessions, "Death Is Not the End," for which Dylan drew on
Revelation, the final book of the New Testament.

While in Nashville for a concert less than two months after *Down
in the Groove*'s release, Dylan wandered into the Country Music
Hall of Fame. Chris Skinker, the museum's curator, remembers his
visit well. "He dropped by out of the blue one summer morning,"
said Skinker. "My boss said to me, 'Chris, don't flip out, but
Dylan's upstairs.'" She eventually spotted him, about a third of the
way through the museum, and noticed he was with his guitarist,
G.E. Smith. "He was explaining fact after fact, detail after detail, to
G.E. Smith. It was almost like he was trying to get across to G.E.,
you know, like 'you need to know this'—that kind of an attitude."
In fact, she thought Dylan would have made a far better tour
guide than most of the people who were employed there at
the time.

At her boss's behest, she finally approached Dylan and invited
him to go downstairs and visit their archives. "You've got Gram
Parsons' guitar," Dylan remarked; she informed him that it was on

loan from Emmylou Harris. Dylan then asked where he could get a good vintage guitar locally. Skinker said the place to go would be Gruhn's Guitars, which was, she reminded him, "right around the corner from the Ryman Auditorium," where he had performed on Johnny Cash's TV show back in 1969. When it became clear that people were flowing into the museum (tourists were regularly dropped off by buses) Dylan said he was running short on time. Sensing some uneasiness, she led him out a back door—but not before he managed to visit the gift shop, purchasing "every book [they] had on Jimmie Rodgers and some Jimmie Rodgers CDs too." Skinker described Dylan as "very affable, very nice and easy to deal with."[64]

In October 1988, Dylan began an unusual one-man campaign to get Amnesty International to include "In the Garden" on the next Amnesty-sponsored tour. The 1988 Amnesty tour, a fourteen-date tour that spanned the globe over a six-week period, concluded on October 15. More than a million people on five continents had heard the tour's message, which drew attention to human rights violations.

The night before the Amnesty tour ended, Dylan told an audience in Upper Darby, Pennsylvania, how honored he was that the human rights organization had chosen two of his songs—"I Shall Be Released" in 1986 and "Chimes of Freedom" in 1988—to close their show. Then he expressed his hope that the following year, the group would choose to close their show with "In the Garden"—one of his most blatantly evangelical songs.

Dylan repeated his plea before singing "In the Garden" on each
night of a four-night stand at Radio City Music Hall in New York,
which started on October 16. On the second night, he shared the
information that he thought Amnesty had already chosen
"Jokerman" for the following year's tour, but he was trying to get
them to reverse that decision. To some people, it seemed almost
perverse that amid the publicity of the Amnesty tour, Dylan would
focus so much attention on his Bible-thumping song from *Saved*.

1989

One who apparently considered Dylan's allegiance to Jesus to be
perverse was Dylan biographer Bob Spitz. He endorsed the idea
that a Jew shouldn't believe in Jesus and was clearly puzzled by
Dylan's conversion in 1979: "Jesus was a concept for the gentiles.
He was their Son of God, their Messiah. He walked on water and
raised bodies from the dead. Jews weren't supposed to believe all
that hocus pocus."[65]

Just prior to the release of his next album, *Oh Mercy*, Dylan granted an interview to Edna Gundersen of *USA Today*. She wondered
what he thought about all the things that had been written about
his personal life. "It's been years since I've read anything about
myself. People can think what they want and let me be," said
Dylan. "You can't let the fame get in the way of your calling.
Everybody is entitled to lead a private life. Then again, God watch-
es everybody, so there's nothing really private, there's nothing we
can hide. As long as you're exposing everything to the power that
created you, people can't uncover too much."

And just days before another appearance on the Chabad telethon, Gundersen reminded Dylan how the press had dubbed him a "born again" in 1979. "If that's what was laid on me, there must have been a reason for it," Dylan replied. "Whatever label is put on you, the purpose of it is to limit your accessibility to people." This paralleled Dylan's comments to Robert Hilburn in 1983, when he called the "born again" label a "media hype term" that "threw people in a corner and left them there."

Gundersen also heard Dylan's take on the "religious content" of *Slow Train Coming, Saved,* and *Shot of Love.* Not surprisingly, he eschewed the label but affirmed the experience. "You'd never hear me saying that stuff is religious one way or the other. To me, it isn't," Dylan said. "It's just based on my experience in daily matters, what you run up against, and how you respond to things. People who work for big companies, that's their 'religion.' That's not a word that has any holiness to it."

She also asked his opinion about the 1960s mantra "Don't trust anyone over thirty." True to form, Dylan dismissed it as a misguided notion, pointing out that about all it accomplished was to sell "a lot of tennis shoes and things people need from the accessory department." All of his musical heroes, he added, were much older than thirty, even back then. "From '66 on, I was trying to raise a family, and that was contrary to the whole epidemic of the '60s. Most people were running away from home and trying to get away from their parents," he said. "That was never intentional on my part, trying to run away from anything. My family was more important to me than any kind of generational '60s thing. Still is. To find some meaning in the '60s for me is real far-fetched…

The '60s will be forgotten. Nostalgia for the '60s is more of a mental thing. It has no ring of reality. It doesn't really have much to do with what's happening today."[66]

The ring of a biblical reality—a fallen, sinful world—could definitely be heard with the release of *Oh Mercy* on September 22, 1989. Its opening track, "Political World," reveals a claustrophobic world where love isn't welcome and crime is rampant but "without a face." It's a world where courage is extinct, children are unwanted, and wisdom is tossed into jail; peace, like love, is also not welcome.

"Everything Is Broken" reveals a common thread that runs throughout Hebrew Scriptures and the New Testament: mankind's fall in the Garden of Eden, through the sin of Adam and Eve. The song lays out a laundry list of broken things: bodies, idols, beds, hearts, words, vows, treaties, laws, rules. Even the animal kingdom isn't immune to the curse: the howl of a hound dog and the croak of the bullfrog point to the same restless, broken creation.

"Disease of Conceit" describes the biblical sin of pride, the sin attributed to Adam and Eve; not even doctors, sings Dylan, have a cure for this human condition. In "Man in the Long Black Coat," a preacher presents a sermon on the condition of the human heart, the truth being that it is futile for people to rely on their own hearts for guidance. The man in the long black coat, coated in dust and filled with impure motives, represents falsehood as he quotes from the Bible. In the end, a woman willingly slips off into the night with him, apparently never to return. Not exactly a toe-tapping tune.

Some respite is found in "Ring Them Bells" as even the heathen
are called to join in the ringing. Dylan's word picture of time and
the bride running backwards alludes to the biblical metaphor for
the bride of Christ—the believers in Jesus who are headed toward
a time when all will be well, as it once was in the Garden of Eden.
St. Peter, upon whose confession Jesus founded His church, is
busy ringing "them bells" so the people will know who God is.
Meanwhile, the sun is going down on the sacred cow, and as the
wayward shepherd sleeps—an image borrowed from the book of
Ezekiel—the mountains fill with lost sheep. "Ring Them Bells"
also expresses the biblical idea of the "chosen few" assisting God
in the judgment of the many when the game of life is finished—
hardly a new theme for Dylan. Ultimately, the heathen are up to
their eyeballs in relativity, busily "breaking down the distance
between right and wrong."

Oh Mercy's closer, "Shooting Star," sums up the album with the
noisy images of engines, bells, and fire trucks from hell juxtaposed
against the silent power of the good folks praying. The end of
time is, no doubt, at hand in this one; in fact, Dylan sings, it's the
"last time you might hear the Sermon on the Mount." It seems no
accident that Dylan chose to parallel the end of time with the
words of Jesus. Toward the end of the Sermon on the Mount,
Jesus spoke about this frightening scenario: "Not everyone who
says to me, 'Lord, Lord,' will enter the kingdom of Heaven, but
only he who does the will of my Father who is in Heaven. Many
will say to me on that day, 'Lord, Lord, did we not prophesy in
your name, and in your name drive out demons and perform
many miracles?' Then I will tell them plainly, 'I never knew you.
Away from me, you evildoers!'" (Matthew 7:21-23 NIV).

Jesus concluded His Sermon on the Mount with a parable, spelling out in no uncertain terms the ultimatum. "Therefore everyone who hears these words of mine, and puts them into practice is like a wise man who built his house on the rock. The rain came down, the streams rose, and the winds blew and beat against that house, yet it did not fall, because it had its foundation on the rock. But everyone who hears these words of mine and does not put them into practice is like a foolish man who built his house on the sand. The rain came down, the streams rose, and the winds blew and beat against that house, and it fell down with a great crash" (Matthew 7:24-27 NIV).

Dylan's *Oh Mercy*, recorded in New Orleans in the spring of 1989, was practically a companion piece to the album of a decade earlier, the Alabama-bred *Slow Train Coming*.

Two days after the release of *Oh Mercy*, Dylan made another appearance on the Chabad telethon, on September 24, 1989, demonstrating that his Jewish roots were obviously still important to him and, of course, fueling further speculation of a Dylan return to Judaism. But Dylan's Amnesty plea eleven months earlier left precious little doubt where Dylan stood regarding his belief in Jesus as the Messiah. In addition, Dylan was singing "In the Garden" in concerts just before his Chabad appearance, as well as afterwards. He was also singing his *Slow Train Coming* songs, including "Gotta Serve Somebody," "I Believe in You," and "When You Gonna Wake Up?" during this same time frame.

As the decade ended, the Berlin Wall fell, fostering hope in a world that otherwise seemed, as Dylan wrote in "Song to Woody" in 1961, to be sick, hungry, tired, and torn.

According to biographer Howard Sounes, around the end of 1989 Dylan revisited his old stomping grounds in New York's Greenwich Village. "Bob called at the apartment of his old friend Dave Van Ronk," he wrote. "Bob complained that young performers did not know traditional music. He added gloomily: 'The devil is the lord of this world.'"[67] This was a New Testament theme that Dylan brought to stages across America at the very beginning of the decade, much to the chagrin of many of his fans. And through his black female singers, he had administered a significant dose of traditional gospel music; in the *Biograph* liner notes, he said he "wanted to expose people to [gospel music] because [he] loved it and it's the real roots of all modern music, but nobody cared."

1990-1994

CHAPTER 6

Reluctant Prophet

In early 1990, while in Paris for a run of concerts, Dylan met up with his friend Leonard Cohen, a poet, songwriter, and recording artist from Montreal. Tom Chaffin, a writer for the *Atlanta Journal-Constitution*, remembers talking with Cohen a few days later. The Jewish poet thought the negative reaction of many longtime fans to Dylan's "religious albums" of 1979-1981 was unfair. He singled out a particular review that asserted *Shot of Love* contained "only one masterpiece"—"Every Grain of Sand." "My God! Only one masterpiece? Does this guy have any idea what it takes to produce a single masterpiece?" lamented Cohen. "I think anything Dylan does merits serious attention."[68]

Back in the States in late February, Dylan made a surprise appearance at a tribute to Roy Orbison in Los Angeles and at a Tom Petty and the Heartbreakers concert in nearby Inglewood on March 1.

Throughout the spring, he was back in the studio, working on *Under the Red Sky*, which would release in September, and *Volume 3* by the Traveling Wilburys, an October release.

Midway through the year, Dylan's faith in God was evident in a letter he sent to Jamie Brown, the editor and founder of *Sister 2 Sister*, a magazine for emerging black female executives in the music industry. The letter, published in the magazine's July issue in honor of their second anniversary, reveals a man constantly on the road, contemplating life, time, and God while traveling the world:

"Life on the road is not what it used to be. But what used to be may not have existed anyway. All of Europe used to be a desert. What they say about shifting sand is not unfounded.

"Everything is happening by the clock. Without clocks there wouldn't be any useful idea of time. My soul is unaware of any time; only in my mind. My poor mind which is so bombarded with dates, calendars and numbers has been deceived into believing there is such a thing as time, woe is me.

"Hasn't everybody, at some point in their life, asked, 'What time is it?' It's no time. The sun comes up and the sun goes down. That's what time it is…

"Reflecting on this, brainwork brings you to the realization that this earth is truly God's footstool and until the entire world believes and obeys the same God, there can be no truth or justice or peace for anyone. The soul never dies and neither does it know time."[69]

This letter explicitly expresses the worldview that there will be no truth, justice, or peace until everyone believes in, and obeys, the same God. Dylan's biblically inspired "When He Returns" touches on this concept: "Truth" is likened to an arrow passing through a narrow gate, recalling Jesus' warning that only a few will enter the narrow gate because of the deceptive appeal of the wide road that leads to destruction; God's "justice" will replace the wrong with the right, and finally true "peace" and the end of wars will only occur when Jesus returns. Dylan's song "Solid Rock" also speaks to this: "People are expecting a false peace to come"; this expresses the worldview that peace will come only when Jesus, the Messiah, returns.

Implicit in Dylan's letter to *Sister 2 Sister* is a monotheistic viewpoint that opposes the multitude of "gods" out there. In Dylan's 1989 song "Ring Them Bells," Saint Peter is ringing "them bells where the four winds blow so the people will know." Dylan sings that the "sun is going down upon the sacred cow." It's safe to assume that the sacred cow here is the biblical metaphor for all false gods. For Dylan, the world will eventually know that there is only one God.

Dylan's reference to the earth as "God's footstool" is also a biblical concept. The psalmist writes, "Exalt the Lord our God and worship at His footstool; Holy is He" (Psalm 99:5, NAS). In the Sermon on the Mount, Jesus repeated the phrase as He spoke to His followers about taking an oath: "I say to you, make no oath at all, either by Heaven, for it is the throne of God, or by the earth, for it is the footstool of His feet, or by Jerusalem, for it is the city of the great king" (Matthew 5:34-35, NAS).

And the prophet Isaiah wrote this: "Thus says the Lord, 'Heaven is My throne, and the earth is My footstool. Where then is a house you could build for Me? And where is a place that I may rest? For My hand made all these things, thus all these things came into being,' declares the Lord. 'But to this one I will look, to him who is humble and contrite of spirit, and who trembles at My word," (Isaiah 66:1-2, NAS).

Several months after sending the letter to *Sister 2 Sister*, Dylan chatted with Edna Gundersen of *USA Today* about the moral state of music. "People say music is intended to elevate the spirit. But you've got a lot of groups and lyrics projecting emptiness and giving you nothing, less than nothing, because they're taking up your time," he said. "It's not difficult to get people throbbing in their guts. That can lead you down an evil path if that's all they're getting. You gotta put something on top of that."[64]

When pressed further about the subject of art, he asked a few rhetorical questions: "What kind of artistry is equal to the silver glisten on a river, or a sunset, or lightning in the sky? What kind of man's artistry can compare to the great artistry of creation?" Dylan, the reflective thinker, was back in his most familiar form. Not long after the interview with Gundersen, Dylan's first album of the 1990s—*Under the Red Sky*—was released. Although it consisted of ten original compositions and boasted a number of big-name artists who contributed to the recording sessions—George Harrison, Elton John, David Crosby, Bruce Hornsby, Al Kooper, Stevie Ray Vaughan, and Slash of Guns n' Roses—the album did not garner positive reviews.

Some of the album's songs, though, were lyrically if not biblically rich. The deceptively simple lyrics of "God Knows" are in fact drawn from the words the psalmist wrote some three thousand years earlier, "For He knows the secrets of the heart" (Psalm 44:21 NAS) and also call up "Gospel Plow" from Dylan's debut album. That song, in its original form (the traditional "Hold On") reminds listeners that in giving Noah the sign of the rainbow, God was warning that fire, not water, would engulf the earth "next time."

Dylan's female singers sang this identical lyric during the gospel tours of 1979-1980 in their version of Charles Johnson's song "It's Gonna Rain." Dylan's lyrics for "God Knows" in 1990 echoed the same sentiment and captured the essence of Genesis 9:8-17, God's promise to Noah and all those who would follow. In addition, the song echoed an admonition given through the apostle Peter, who pointed to this whole business of the "fire next time" with warnings of a brimstone end for those who mock the second coming of Jesus: "But do not let this one fact escape your notice, beloved, that with the Lord one day is as a thousand years, and a thousand years as one day. The Lord is not slow about His promise, as some count slowness, but is patient toward you, not wishing for any to perish but for all to come to repentance. But the day of the Lord will come like a thief, in which the heavens and earth will pass away with a roar and the elements will be destroyed with intense heat, and the earth and its works will be burned up" (2 Peter 3:8-10, NAS).

The "God knows the secrets of your heart" lyric in "God knows" was also foreshadowed a decade earlier when Dylan addressed a gospel tour audience in Worcester, Massachusetts: "Eternal life is yours for the asking. And don't forget, God knows the secrets of your heart. God knows all the secrets. You can't keep nothing from Him. All right, don't you be deceived by the mockers of the truth. Lot of people praying. There's only one way—praying all week, praying all year. God got things in store for you, and I know He's calling to His people now. Some of you out there are nice people, maybe some of you aren't. But in the last days He's gonna pour out His Spirit on all flesh. Now, you know if you're called or not. I know."

"What kind of artistry is equal to the silver glisten on a river or a sunset or lightning in the sky? What kind of man's artistry can compare to the great artistry of creation?"

—1990

Another lyric in "God Knows," one that reminds listeners that they'll leave this world empty-handed, was a premise Dylan certainly wouldn't have disagreed with prior to 1979, but afterwards it seemed to take on a much greater significance. He said this to the same Worcester audience in May 1980: "There's only one thing that can save you, only one person went to the cross for you. And you can take it or leave it. Now if you don't believe in heaven or hell, you're [still] gonna die. You'll find out. Remember now, when you came into this world, what did you bring with you? And what you gonna take with you when you leave? You're not gonna need your baggage, not gonna take your attitudes, not gonna take your prejudices, pride, none of that. You're not gonna take none of that with you. You can't leave with it, you'll go all alone."

1991

During the course of 1991, Dylan sang "Gotta Serve Somebody" in concert more than eighty times, "I Believe in You" twenty-nine times, and "In the Garden" ten times. A decade had passed since the gospel tours, yet Dylan continued to remind some of his audiences—through an occasional stage rap—just what these songs were all about.

At two concerts in Glasgow, Scotland, in February, Dylan told the first night's audience that although "In the Garden" wasn't all that well known, it remained one of his favorite songs. The second night, he referred to "Gotta Serve Somebody" as a gospel song, leaving no wiggle room for those revisionists who over the years had speculated that the song really had nothing to do with Jesus.

But back in the States, Dylan once again raised a few eyebrows with his off-handed, on-stage remarks to several Massachusetts audiences a few months later. In those concerts, and in others that followed, he called both "In the Garden" and "Gotta Serve Somebody" his "anti-religion" songs.

To just about anyone outside the evangelical fold, comments like that would either add to the already monumental and confusing Dylan mystique or serve to confirm that he had renounced the faith he claimed to have found in 1979. But what was he really saying? There's little question that he was debunking the misconception that he had turned to "religion" rather than to Jesus. To Dylan, as it is to most evangelical Christians, the distinction is a crucial one.

In an evangelical context, faith in Jesus involves being in an active and vital relationship with Him. It has little or nothing to do with the contemporary understanding of the word "religion," which has come to signify faith in a certain creed or set of doctrines and rituals. To evangelicals—the segment of Christianity through which Dylan came into a relationship with Jesus—religion, unlike Jesus, strips people of any possibility of a dynamic faith in a living God.

What's more, even a cursory reading of the Gospels reveals just how often Jesus exposed the corruption and blindness of the religious leaders of His day. He reserved His most scathing remarks for some of the Pharisees—think of them as the ultra-fundamentalists of first-century Judaism—even as He lavished love and compassion on those people that the Pharisees were leading astray. There's little doubt that this is the kind of life-robbing religion Dylan was referring to in his concerts; apart from this context, it would make no sense for him to call "Gotta Serve Somebody" a gospel song on one occasion and an anti-religion song several months later.

Then too, both songs point the finger at religious leaders. "Gotta Serve Somebody" includes in its laundry list of humanity "preachers with your spiritual pride"—the Pharisees of the contemporary church. "In the Garden" shines the spotlight on those religious leaders—the chief priests—who tracked Jesus down as He prayed in the Garden of Gethsemane and arrested Him.

In the end, there seems to be little doubt that Dylan's 1991 stage raps simply affirmed the reality of his experience with Jesus back in 1979.

On May 24, 1991, Dylan's fiftieth birthday, Senator Joe Lieberman wished the singer a happy birthday from the floor of the Senate. Dylan, he pointed out, was the one who years before had heralded the changes that would subsequently take place in the world, continuing to play his music "as society erupted in great social ferment, matching the power of words with the power of music." In an unanticipated but accurate assessment of the singer, Lieberman added: "There is a mystery to Bob Dylan, which is surprising, in a way, given how freely he has expressed himself through his music. But the mystery results, I think, from Dylan's refusal to play roles society might seek to assign him—roles like superstar, rock idol, prophet...He offers us nothing more—and nothing less—than his music." And with that, he publicly thanked Dylan for the words and songs that had meant so much to him over the years.

On September 15, 1991, with guitar in hand, Dylan appeared for the third time on Chabad's annual telethon, this time alongside old friend Kinky Friedman for a performance of "Sold American." As they belted out Friedman's song, both donned black cowboy hats. Prior to the song, Dylan spoke to the audience, encouraged people to contribute, and thanked the rabbis who were present.

What this seemed to mean—and some Dylan-observers are ever-vigilant regarding the underlying "meaning" of his every move—was that Dylan had absolutely no problem embracing both his Jewish heritage and a good cause. Some might see this as spiritual schizophrenia, considering that throughout this same year Dylan was trotting out his gospel songs in his concerts. But anyone who reaches that conclusion would simply reveal his own ignorance of Dylan's spiritual history, the interviews he's given, and what it might mean for a Jewish person to believe in Jesus.

And that final factor—how a Jewish person can believe in Jesus and still be Jewish—is perhaps the one that ultimately gets to the heart of Dylan's spiritual journey.

Until the Jesus Movement of the 1970s and the subsequent rise of ministries like Jews for Jesus, any Jewish person who believed that Jesus was the long-awaited Messiah generally kept a low profile, most often continuing to publicly participate in synagogue activities while privately worshiping Jesus Christ at home. Then the Jesus Movement threw the doors of worship wide open, and a number of Messianic Jewish ministries—those that adhere to the belief that Jesus is the Messiah—began to grow. Young Jews who had long ago abandoned the religion of their families suddenly discovered Jesus and, with Him, a newfound appreciation for their Jewish heritage. The Messianic Jewish ministries attracted so many new converts that they eventually became a force to be reckoned with.

After a heady honeymoon phase, though, many in the church who had initially embraced their Jewish brothers and sisters became suspicious of Messianic Jews, labeling them Judaizers and charging them with polluting the gospel by allegedly insisting that their converts become more Jewish than they had ever been before. Now many Jewish believers in Jesus found themselves shunned by both Christians and Jews.

It was amid this environment of distrust and isolation that Bob Dylan the Jew became a Christian in 1979. Even though his involvement with any single Messianic Jewish ministry was incidental at best, he almost certainly had to be aware of the tension between those ministries and the gentile church. In typical Dylan fashion, he apparently ignored the bickering and went on with his spiritual life, no doubt experiencing his Jewishness on a far deeper level than he had at any time since his bar mitzvah.

Then, too, he'd had his own brand of rejection to deal with, not only from the Jewish community, which saw his conversion as religious betrayal, but also from a music industry that wanted its poster boy for the counterculture to get over his silly flirtation with Christianity and get back to the business of creating the kind of music it expected from him.

It's no wonder that as late as 1991, a dozen years after his initial encounter with Jesus, Bob Dylan continued to sing "I Believe in You," with its telling lyrics: "And they look at me and frown / They'd like to drive me from this town / They don't want me around / Because I believe in you...I believe in you even though I be outnumbered / Oh, though the earth may shake me / Oh, though my friends forsake me / Oh, even that couldn't make me go back."[70] With hundreds of songs in his repertoire, Dylan could have easily left this one out. It's highly unlikely he would have continued to sing it unless he continued to believe it.

Toward the end of 1991, Robert Hilburn of the *Los Angeles Times* asked Dylan about his cultural impact as an artist. "There's no one to my knowledge that isn't surprised by their longevity, including myself, but it's very dangerous to plan [far ahead], because you are just dealing with your vanity," Dylan said. "Tomorrow is hard enough. It's God who gives you the freedom, and the days you should be most concerned with are today and tomorrow."[71]

1992

Dylan may have been the reluctant prophet, but the songs he chose to sing often seemed to express his allegiances. Take, for example, his summer 1992 recording sessions with a fellow Jew, his friend David Bromberg. Included in those sessions was Dallas Holm's "Rise Again," a song Dylan sang in concert in 1980 and 1981.

Holm's recording is still a staple on contemporary Christian radio, and the song's lyrics are about as Christian as you can get: "Go ahead, drive the nails in My hands, laugh at Me where I stand…There's no power on earth can tie Me down / Yes I'll rise again—death can't keep Me in the ground / Go ahead and mock My name—My love for you is still the same…'Cause I'll come again—there's no power on earth can keep Me back / Yes I'll come again—come to take My people back / Go ahead and say I'm dead and gone / But you will see that you were wrong."[72]

For a man who has always lived by and sung his convictions, the recording of "Rise Again" offers another clear indication of where Dylan was coming from at the time.

November of 1992 saw the release of *Good As I Been to You*, an album consisting of thirteen cover songs and no bells and whistles—just Dylan's voice accompanied by his acoustic guitar on these old standards. One of the songs, Big Joe Williams' "Sittin' on Top of the World," wasn't unfamiliar territory for Dylan, since in the spring of 1962 Dylan had provided back-up vocals on the song for Victoria Spivey and Big Joe himself for her album, *Victoria Spivey: Three Kings and a Queen*.

Good As I Been to You marked the first Dylan album entirely composed of cover songs (not including the infamous release of 1973's *Dylan: A Fool Such As I*). The seed for the project was certainly planted years before as Dylan had, in 1985, shared this with Cameron Crowe: "I guess I'd like to do a concept album like, you know, [Willie Nelson's] *Red Headed Stranger* or something, maybe a children's album, or an album of cover songs, but I don't know if the people would let me get away with that: 'A Million Miles From Nowhere,' 'I Who Have Nothing,' 'All My Tomorrows,' 'I'm in the Mood For Love,' 'More Than You Know,' 'It's a Sin to Lie'…I guess someday I'd like to do an album of standards, also, maybe instrumentals, guitar melodies with percussion; people don't know I can do that sort of thing. I can get away with a lot more in a show than I can on record." Seven years after these comments, Bob Dylan, via *Good As I Been to You*, "got away" with an album of just covers and standards.

As for Dylan's original song output, critics, reviewers, and even the public have labored under the misconception that Dylan stopped writing biblically-inspired songs around 1982. But an analysis of Dylan's lyrics by author Bert Cartwright, whose book *The Bible in the Lyrics of Bob Dylan* was updated in 1992, indicates that quite the opposite is true. Acknowledging that Dylan's songwriting output had decreased, Cartwright, a pastor and Dylan fan from Forth Worth, Texas, pointed out that the number of biblical allusions in his compositions had markedly increased. According to the author, sixty-seven of the eighty-eight songs Dylan wrote between 1979 and 1990 contained references to Scripture—by his count, a total of 459 biblical references.

1993

After the European tour in early 1993, Dylan appeared at a few U.S. venues in the South. In June he revisited the Holy Land, performing before crowds in Tel Aviv, Beersheba, and Haifa. Perhaps the most interesting event of the visit took place in Jerusalem when he and the band visited the Western Wall early one morning, accompanied by an Israeli policeman toting a submachine gun.[73]

Apparently unscathed by the incident, Dylan left Israel to tour southern Europe, returning in late July to the States, where he began a cross-country tour. In October, *World Gone Wrong* was released, giving Dylan another opportunity to talk about his faith. In the liner notes to "Lone Pilgrim," he explained why he chose to sing Doc Watson's version of the song: "What attracts me to the song is how the lunacy of trying to fool the self is set aside at some given point. Salvation and the needs of mankind are prominent and hegemony takes a breathing spell. 'My soul flew to mansions on high.' Technology to wipe out truth is now available. Not everybody can afford it but it's available. When the cost comes down, look out!" The lyric, "My soul flew to mansions on high" owes a debt to the words of Jesus: "In My Father's house are many mansions; if it were not so, I would have told you. I go to prepare a place for you" (John 14:2 NKJV).

When talking about what Frank Hutchinson's old song "Stack a Lee" meant to him, Dylan asserted that no man will gain immortality through public acclaim and then summarily dismissed ego-

---

"There's no one to my knowledge that isn't surprised by their longevity, including myself, but it's very dangerous to plan [far ahead], because you are just dealing with your vanity. Tomorrow is hard enough. It's God who gives you he freedom, and the days you should be most concerned with are today and tomorrow."

—1991

ism, existentialism, and Dionysus with disdain. In addition, to hear Dylan label the phrase "alternative lifestyle" a scam makes it tempting to connect the dots with his infamous comments at the Hartford concert of 1980 regarding a certain "political party" in San Francisco, the active homosexual lobby. Whatever the case, for 1993 ears, Dylan turned the meaning of this contemporary phrase—"alternative lifestyle"—on its head, insisting that a "true alternative lifestyle" would involve something like idle gang members becoming productive farm hands. If nothing else, this represented a charming solution to urban blight and testified to Dylan's enduring wit.

The liner notes to "Delia" include a theological reference, as Dylan describes a character he sees in the song: "He's not interested in mosques on the temple mount, Armageddon or World War III, doesn't put his face in his knees & weep & wears no dunce hat, makes no apology & is doomed to obscurity." In typical Dylan fashion, a traditional love-gone-wrong song like "Delia" evoked no less than the grave issues of the ongoing conflict in the Middle East, his Jewish roots, and prophetic scenarios in the Bible.

As for the songs on *World Gone Wrong*, Dylan had once again returned to the folk and blues roots of his first album much like he did on the previous year's release of *Good As I Been to You*. The sound of the new album was another bare-bones approach—the simple yet powerful combination of Dylan's voice, his phrasing, and a trusty acoustic guitar. Just cover versions or traditional songs—take it or leave it. Dylan shared the fact that he learned "Two Soldiers" from Jerry Garcia and that "Blood in My Eyes" and "World Gone Wrong" were influenced by the Mississippi Sheiks, a country and blues string band popular in the twenties and thirties.

Dylan's thoughts on the title track made the song appear to con-
stitute a sad update on the motley crew of "Desolation Row"—evil
charlatans espousing their respective gobbledygook, the phony
parades filing down the lonely streets and limited-access high-
ways, the legendary bimbos and bozos. Perhaps their eyes had
wandered too far away from Noah's rainbow and their ears had
turned off the Sermon on the Mount. The combination of the
songs and Dylan's explanation of them was a formidable one-two
punch. Predictably, though, some grumbled at the fact that there
were no "new" Dylan songs on the album.

In an interview with Gary Hill of the Reuters News Service in early
October, Dylan described *World Gone Wrong* as an "underground"
effort that offered the kind of truth-telling, "roots" music that
young people were hungering for. "There are young people who
are fed up with what they hear," said Dylan. Pop radio didn't play
the music he cared about, and he considered the current crop of
country singers to be "polluted and unclean" because they had
strayed so far from their hillbilly roots. Although Hill couldn't pin
him down to identify his personal brand of religion, Dylan did
say that he was glad that God had still been present in the schools
when he was growing up.

"A person without faith is like a walking corpse," remarked Dylan.
"And now people have to fight to get the faith back, especially
in schools."

1994

Dylan began touring again in early 1994, starting with eleven concerts in Japan, then returning to the States in April and May.
During the tour, Ellen Futterman of the *St. Louis Post-Dispatch*
interviewed Dylan, broaching the "legend" issue: "Having had
three decades to adjust, are you more comfortable being a living
legend?" "I try to be an illuminated person," said Dylan. "Nobody
should put anyone on a pedestal—it really can damage a person's
mentality and lead to ignorance. At that point, a person ceases to
be a person." Dylan's friend T-Bone Burnett once spoke along
similar lines when interviewed by *L.A. Weekly* back in 1982: "To
idolize a person is to murder him in a sense. You take away his
humanity."

Several months later when Dylan resumed his U.S. tour after a
brief round of concerts in Europe, Tony Norman, a columnist for
the *Pittsburgh Post-Gazette*, captured this spirit of idolatry while
attending a concert in 1994: "Dylan performed his moving medi-
tation on the passion of Jesus, 'In the Garden,' and turned what
was already a fairly rowdy audience into an ecstatic mob at an
open-air revival meeting: 'Did they know He was the Son of God /
Did they know He was Lord?' Maybe the sold-out audience didn't
know that He was the Lord, but they were pretty sure that Bob
Dylan came close."

During a touring hiatus in September, Dylan wrote the foreword
to his book of drawings, *Drawn Blank*. Consisting mostly of pencil
sketches, they were composed over a few years between 1989 and
1992 "in various locations mainly to relax and refocus a restless

mind," he wrote.[72] A cross appeared in the backdrop of one of his sketches, with "Jesus" inscribed on the horizontal beam and "Saves" inscribed on the vertical beam. In an age in which Dylan asserts "We all gotta serve somebody," perhaps this reminder of redemption served to relax and refocus a restless mind accustomed to a landscape that seemed to include only those vistas that could be seen from inside a tour bus or hotel room or hideaway. Soon enough, he would be back on the road, touring the U.S. throughout October and early November before returning to the studio for a series of recording sessions for *MTV Unplugged*.

1995-1998

CHAPTER 7
Serve Somebody

In September 1995, John Dolen, a journalist for Fort Lauderdale's *Sun-Sentinel*, asked Dylan how he felt about certain lyrics from "Precious Angel," a song from *Slow Train Coming* ("You talk about Buddha / You talk about Muhammad / But you never said a word about the One who came to die for us instead"). "Just writing a song like that probably emancipated me from other kind of illusions," said Dylan. "I can't say that I would disagree with that line. On its own level, it was some kind of turning point for me, writing that."

Dolen concluded the interview by asking if Dylan still saw a slow train coming, an obvious reference to the Second Coming as reflected in Dylan's album *Slow Train Coming*. "When I look ahead now it's picked up quite a bit of speed," said Dylan. "In fact, it's going like a freight train now."

In the aftermath of his midnight telephone interview with Dylan, Dolen wrote about the experience for *On the Tracks*: "The final impression I have of him is that at times he spoke like a prophet, with that elliptical logic reminiscent of the biblical teachers, and that same sense of cutting to the core meaning of things. He did all this without pretense, without affectation, and with professional respect for where I was coming from."[74]

A week after his chat with Dolen, Dylan reportedly ambled into a Yom Kippur service at the Temple Beth El synagogue in West Palm Beach, Florida. "You would have thought Elijah had come through the door as worshippers who recognized him did double takes," wrote Scott Benarde of the *Jewish Journal*. "Say what you want about Bob 'Robert Zimmerman' Dylan's late 1970s experience as a born-again Christian, the enigmatic superstar's real roots were showing. Dylan's synagogue appearance made the local papers. It also made local Jews proud. It did not make national news, which is probably how Dylan, who likes maintaining an air of mystery, preferred it."[75]

Just four nights before his synagogue visit, Dylan sang "I Believe in You" in concert. Three nights later, Dylan included "In the Garden" in a concert on the heels of Yom Kippur; the song remains the strongest argument yet, according to Larry Yudelson, who runs a website that focuses on the singer's Jewish roots, that Dylan has not "decisively abandoned Christianity."[76]

1996

By the spring of 1996, *Mojo* magazine ran an interview with Mark Knopfler in which the Dire Straits guitarist was asked about his collaborations with Dylan. "I've always felt protective of Bob. The first time I met him I felt like putting my arm around his shoulders because...I think he's always had a difficult life, being virtually deified since he was a kid," said Knopfler. "I remember one night when we were recording *Slow Train Coming* at Muscle Shoals. Some fans camped outside the studio and when we came out, this guy approached him with these [Charles] Manson eyes. It was okay. Bob said a few words. [But] it's just difficult [for him]."

Before the year's end, Chris Skinker, who had met Dylan in 1988 at the Country Music Hall of Fame, helped compile a guest list for a party for musician Ralph Stanley to be held in commemoration of his fifty-year career. The Country Music Hall of Fame would be rented out for the occasion. She knew Dylan to be a big fan of Stanley's music, and before long, she received a phone call from Dylan's management. Then, Dylan himself sent a telegram to Stanley that read, "Dr. Stanley, The fields have turned to brown, but you have not. Congratulations on 50 years. Bob Dylan." This impressed Skinker for three reasons: first, Dylan used the term of endearment for the legendary bluegrass singer, "Dr. Stanley"; second, he quoted a Stanley song in the telegram; and third, he seemed adamant about being represented at this party even though he couldn't make it. She contrasted Dylan's gesture of respect with the disappointment she felt after more than a few big names in country music failed to even RSVP for the event. Little did she know, within a year she would have another opportunity to meet Dylan: Stanley and Dylan would be collaborating in a recording studio.[77]

"This one phrase was going through my head:
'Work while the day lasts, because the night of death cometh
when no man can work.' I don't recall
where I heard it. I like preaching, I hear a lot of preaching,
and I probably just heard it somewhere. Maybe it's
in the Psalms, it beats me. But it wouldn't let me go."

—1997

"I must work the works of Him who sent me, while it is day: the
night cometh, when no man can work.
As long as I am in the world, I am the light of the world."

—Jesus, circa 33 A.D., Jerusalem

1997

On May 21, 1997, Dylan participated in a charity benefit for the
Simon Wiesenthal Center, an organization that supports a
museum and offers educational programs on the atrocities of the
Holocaust and the importance of tolerance. According to Robert
Eshman of the *Jewish Journal*, Dylan "sang three songs, beautifully,
coherently, acoustically, ending with 'Forever Young.' Then he
was gone, like a dream, leaving, by his decree, no pictures and
no video."

Four days after the Simon Wiesenthal performance, Dylan was
hospitalized after complaining of severe chest pains. The official
diagnosis was pericarditis, an inflammation of the protective
covering that surrounds the heart. Doctors prescribed medication
and rest; meanwhile, wild rumors about the state of Dylan's
health began to circulate, reporting that he had suffered a heart
attack or that he had died. The illness is potentially fatal only
in rare cases that involve massive infection, which Dylan did
not develop.

Following his release from the hospital, Dylan issued a statement
to *Time* magazine that said, "I really thought I'd be seeing Elvis
soon." Alan Jacobs, writing for *Books & Culture: A Christian Review*,
observed that this remark "in its substitution of Elvis for Jesus is
both a witty reflection on American culture's uncertainty about
the identity of the true King and a tantalizing comment on
Dylan's own religious pilgrimage."

Within a few months, rumors abounded that Dylan would be singing before the pope as an invited guest at the World Eucharistic Congress, an annual week-long event that culminates in a concert. Three weeks before the scheduled event, Dylan gave *Time* magazine another wry comment: "The pope, huh? I guess if the Vatican is reporting it, it must be happening."

On September 27, 1997, several hundred thousand people, including Pope John Paul II, attended the concert in Bologna, Italy. Only an overactive imagination would conclude that Dylan's appearance implied an official "endorsement" of Catholicism or of the pope himself, as others concluded about his endorsement of Judaism each time he visited a synagogue. But certainly the historical figure of Jesus, and the symbolism of His body and blood—which loomed behind this Eucharistic week—were not only familiar to Dylan but, arguably, also very personal to him.

According to *People Weekly*, "despite objections from Vatican critics, one of whom labeled Dylan a communist, the Pope reportedly chose the aging rocker to perform." There would be all manner of interpretations and commentary on why Dylan was there in the first place. "The Church welcomes whatever is true and beautiful and good," said Ernest Vecchi, an event organizer and vicar in the Bologna archdiocese. "Bob Dylan is one of the best representatives of a highly poetic and spiritual rock music, and I believe he has recently moved closer to Christianity."[78]

Queen Esther Marrow, a gospel singer who recorded and toured with Dylan between 1985 and 1987, opened the Bologna concert and was followed by the Harlem Gospel Singers and others. A chorus of Catholic youth then recited Dylan's "Forever Young" in Italian, a performance that drew papal applause. Following several other performances, including one by tenor Andrea Bocelli, the youth reappeared and recited the lyrical questions posed by Dylan's "Blowin' in the Wind." The pope then launched into a twenty-minute sermon that could have passed for a Dylan stage rant of 1979 or 1980, one that clearly defined the exclusive nature of Christianity: "You've asked me, 'How many roads must a man walk down before he becomes a man?'...I answer you, 'One!' There is only one road for a man, and it is Christ, who said, 'I am the Life.'"

The pope's comments echoed Dylan's own words to a 1979 audience in Albuquerque, New Mexico: "I told you 'The Times They Are A-Changin',' and they did. I said the answer was 'Blowin' in the Wind,' and it was. I'm telling you now Jesus is coming back, and He is. And there is no other way of salvation...There's only one way to believe, there's only one Way, the Truth and the Life. It took a long time to figure that out before it did come to me, and I hope it doesn't take you that long."

Dylan's set in Bologna consisted of "Knockin' on Heaven's Door," "A Hard Rain's A-Gonna Fall," and "Forever Young." Following an electric version of "A Hard Rain's A-Gonna Fall"— the first since the final show of the 1981 gospel tour—the fifty-six-year-old singer greeted the pope and shook his hand.

"Before the last song Dylan took off his cowboy hat, went up to the podium where the pope sat in his chair, greeted him and engaged in some conversation," noted longtime followers Mike

Wyvill and John Wraith. "So there was Dylan, playing for the Pope in an event sponsored by Volkswagen live on TV. Weird."[79] When Dylan was later asked about the concert, Murray Engleheart of *Guitar World* wondered if Dylan intended any irony in playing "Knockin' on Heaven's Door," given the venue. "No, because that's the song they wanted to hear," he replied. "It seemed to be a good correspondence to the situation."

As Dylan flew into Nashville on a stormy November 30, 1997, en route to a studio, the song he thought he would be singing with Ralph Stanley was "Riding the Midnight Train." Meanwhile, Chris Skinker, the production assistant for the recording session, remembers nervously watching the weather forecasts on TV in the studio control room. She vividly remembers storms pounding against the studio walls and the fact that tornado warnings were being issued in the area. Then, an unexpected knock on the studio door came as an early-arriving Dylan, "dressed to the nines," stood there in the pouring wind and rain. With the aid of an umbrella, Skinker escorted him in and offered to take his coat and bring him something to drink. As Dylan dried off, he listened to Stanley and his band rehearsing "Riding the Midnight Train." At the last minute, Dylan had a change of heart and wanted to sing, instead, "The Lonesome River." According to Skinker, the decision prompted a mad scramble to get both the song's lyrics and the band lined up.

But what really stood out in her mind was the moment she introduced Dylan to Ralph Stanley. Dylan took off his hat, an action she viewed as a respectful gesture of deference to an elder and evidence of a man who was reared well. From the moment Dylan walked into the studio, he displayed nothing but the utmost respect for Stanley. "Ralph Stanley and Bob Dylan are the two people that most influenced me musically, and they really connected," said Skinker.

"I believe Bob Dylan wanted to record with me and I wanted him to record with me, too, you see," said Stanley. "And this engineer down in Nashville did all the correspondence and everything, but I was very glad that Bob decided to record with me. And I think he was a lot of help on the record [*Clinch Mountain Country: Ralph Stanley & Friends*, 1998]."[80] For his part, Dylan called it no less than "the highlight of his career."[81]

But author Tim Riley, who didn't see too many highlights in the Dylan chronology when he updated his book, *Hard Rain: A Dylan Commentary* in 1999, was apparently still reeling from the fact that Dylan performed at the U.S. Military Academy at West Point in 1990 and accepted the Lifetime Achievement Grammy in 1991. He found it unbearable that in 1997 Dylan performed at "the Vatican" and two months later accepted the "Congressional Medal of Honor"—some significant errors on Riley's part, since Dylan's performance was not at the Vatican but in Bologna, and since the Congressional Medal of Honor is awarded only to soldiers who display valor in action against an enemy force.

What Riley was referring to was the Kennedy Center Honors, held a week after Dylan's duet with Ralph Stanley. President Clinton held a reception in the East Room of the White House for the five honorees—Charlton Heston, Lauren Bacall, Jessye Norman, Edward Villella, and Bob Dylan—at which he made these comments about Dylan: "He probably had more impact on people of my generation than any other creative artist. His voice and lyrics haven't always been easy on the ear, but throughout his career Bob Dylan has never aimed to please. He's disturbed the peace and discomforted the powerful...'Like a Rolling Stone,' Bob Dylan has kept moving forward, musically and spiritually, challenging all of us to move forward with him. Thank you, Bob Dylan, for a lifetime of stirring the conscience of a nation."

Newt Gingrich, the Speaker of the U.S. House of Representatives—and the political polar opposite of Clinton—added a few words about the honor bestowed on Dylan. "The sheer magic, for I think everyone in my generation, is to finally have our nation recognize Bob Dylan," he said.

Among the family members accompanying Dylan to the Kennedy Center Honors program were his mother, then eighty-two years old, and Ethel Crystal, his aunt, the woman who introduced Beatty to Abraham Zimmerman at a New Year's party in Duluth, Minnesota, more than six decades earlier. The honorees and their families were seated in the same balcony where, a few feet away, a couple of noted Washingtonians, Bill and Hillary Clinton, were seated.

The show concluded with Shirley Caesar's impassioned cover of Dylan's "Gotta Serve Somebody," which she had also covered on her 1980 album, *Rejoice*. Five years later, Dylan confessed to Cameron Crowe that he liked her version of "Gotta Serve Somebody" better than his.

At the Kennedy Center, Caesar launched into her customized introduction of the song: "In the twenty-fourth chapter of Joshua, about the fifteenth verse, I heard Joshua say…" During the singing of the song she added the gospel invitation: "Make up in your mind and come on the Lord's side." She also called forth Dylan's 1979 profession of faith, "I heard Bob Dylan say, 'It might be the Devil, let it be the Lord; you gotta serve somebody." Then Caesar, along with her backup singers, concluded the song with what the lyrics, no doubt, imply—"Serve my Jesus…Jesus!"

You have to wonder how all this went over with Dylan's Aunt Ethel, who later shared her thoughts on Dylan's conversion with biographer Howard Sounes: "I think it was for publicity, that's what I think. Because he is Jewish-minded, plenty Jewish-minded," she said. "He was brought up that way. He was bar mitzvahed."[82]

Yet there are Jews like Ruth Rosen who believe the New Testament to be very "Jewish-minded" and a book worthy of serious consideration. "We [Jews who believe in Jesus] see nothing in the New Testament that is non-Jewish or anti-Jewish. It is, to the contrary, woven with the warp and woof of Jewish hope and prophetic promise," she writes in her book *Jesus for Jews*. "If one can accept the revelation of Moses and the prophets with utter seriousness, there should be nothing really strange in the New Testament. The real challenge of the New Testament, as we see it, is not about Jewishness, but about faith. It is not a question of, 'Is it Jewish?' We believe that careful investigation will verify its Jewishness. The real question is, 'Is it true?' That, as we have stated, is really a question of faith and it holds a challenge for all people, Jew and Gentile alike."[83]

That the New Testament was on Dylan's "Jewish mind" became evident as he discussed his songwriting endeavors with Jon Pareles of the *New York Times* in 1997. During the interview, Dylan referred to a certain phrase that kept running through his head, a phrase that wouldn't leave him alone: "Environment affects me a great deal...A lot of the songs [from *Time Out of Mind*] were written after the sun went down. And I like storms. I like to stay up during a storm," said Dylan. "I get very meditative sometimes, and this one phrase was going through my head: 'Work while the day lasts, because the night of death cometh when no man can work.' I don't recall where I heard it. I like preaching, I hear a lot of preaching, and I probably just heard it somewhere. Maybe it's in the Psalms, it beats me. But it wouldn't let me go. I was, like, what does that phrase mean? But it was at the forefront of my mind, for a long period of time, and I think a lot of that is instilled into this record."[84]

The sixteen words at "the forefront" of Dylan's mind—"Work while the day lasts, because the night of death cometh when no man can work"—indeed had their origins in a biblical passage, one where Jesus gives sight to a man who has been blind since birth. The Gospel of John relates this story: "And as Jesus passed by, He saw a man who was blind from his birth. And His disciples asked him, saying, 'Master, who did sin, this man, or his parents, that he was born blind?' Jesus answered, 'Neither hath this man sinned, nor his parents: but that the works of God should be made manifest in him. I must work the works of Him who sent me, while it is day: the night cometh, when no man can work. As long as I am in the world, I am the light of the world'" (John 9:1-6, KJV).

Dylan's comments regarding *Time Out of Mind* certainly did not mark the first time he alluded to the biblical elements in his songs. In 1985, he told Bill Flanagan about the influence of the Bible on his songwriting; his songs, he said, always came back to that influence. In the same year, he told Cameron Crowe that he listened mostly to "preacher stations"; in 1986, Mikal Gilmore heard Dylan assert that the Bible was the only thing that he knew that "stayed true." God was the ultimate truth and what ultimately sustained him in a world gone wrong. And if God not only oversaw but also ordained the writing of the Bible, then the implication is obvious: God is the only faithful one.

There is no doubt that much of the shadowy music in America's past, from the slave spirituals to the gospel songs of rural America, are steeped in the Good Book. People just couldn't escape the God of time and space, who, although at times seemed absent, was simply hidden in the shadows working out His will—or was revealing Himself so clearly that folks either had to drop on bended knee or turn their hearts away.

"Those old songs are my lexicon and my prayer book...All my beliefs come out of those old songs, literally, anything from 'Let Me Rest on That Peaceful Mountain' to 'Keep on the Sunny Side,'" Dylan told Jon Pareles. "You can find all my philosophy in those old songs. I believe in a God of time and space, but if people ask me about that, my impulse is to point them back toward those songs. I believe in Hank Williams singing 'I Saw the Light.' I've seen the Light, too."

"Let Me Rest on That Peaceful Mountain" is a lyric from a Ralph

Stanley song written in honor of his late brother Carter, who died in 1966. Stanley's childlike faith is evident in the lyrics that express trust in God and a longing for heaven—themes that are not exactly foreign to Dylan's own work. "Keep on the Sunny Side," an A.P. Carter song, refers specifically to the Savior—Jesus.

In 1997, Dylan told David Gates of *Newsweek*, "I don't adhere to rabbis, preachers, evangelists, all of that. I've learned more from the songs than I've learned from any of this kind of entity. The songs are my lexicon. I believe the songs." Dylan, a curious creature of contradictions, said this just after maintaining a few days earlier that he liked to listen to preaching. But maybe this isn't a contradiction after all. Dylan may have been distancing himself from the appearance of following any one preacher. More likely, Dylan simply is reminded of transcendent biblical truths through songs rather than sermons.

It seems clear that Dylan doesn't believe any human being can provide salvation for another human being's soul. "The basic thing, I feel, is to get in touch with Christ yourself. He will lead you," he told Robert Hilburn of the *Los Angeles Times* in 1980. "Any preacher who is a real preacher will tell you that: 'Don't follow me, follow Christ.'"

The new material released in 1997, the songs from *Time Out of Mind*, included the bluesy "Standing in the Doorway," in which Dylan hears the church bells ringing in the yard as he wonders who they're ringing for. There are things he could say, but doesn't; he knows "the mercy of God must be near." In "Cold Irons Bound," another blues-drenched song, the singer confesses, "I went to church on Sunday / As she passed by / My love for her has taken such a long time to die." Not long after Dylan recorded these songs, biographer Howard Sounes discovered a building complex in Santa Monica, California, that Dylan owned. It included a private gymnasium, private and public offices, a public coffeehouse, and "paradoxically, for a Jew who had famously become a Christian, Bob leased the adjacent meeting hall for use as a synagogue."

Although Dylan's *Time Out of Mind* expressed a fair amount of sorrow and suffering, it was not without hope. In "Til I Fell In Love With You," God is Dylan's "shield"; because of this Dylan concludes, "He won't lead me astray." But the threads of faith and hope in *Time Out of Mind* and the usual biblical allusions were generally overlooked by the press.

"The album manages to skip the twentieth century," wrote Alex Ross of *The New Yorker*. "People ride in buggies, trains discourage gambling, there's no air-conditioning ('It's too hot to sleep'), church bells ring, 'gay' means 'happy,' the time of day is measured by the sun, lamps apparently run on gas (and are turned 'down low'), and, most of the time, the singer is walking. The wistfulness is intense. The singer is in love with a musical past that's gone forever."

Dylan didn't like the characterization of *Time Out of Mind* as bitter, dark, and lonely. "I don't agree at all; what's happening in Bosnia or in South America, that's bitter," he told *Der Spiegel*. "It's certainly not an album of felicity," he added in an interview with Robert Hilburn of the *Los Angeles Times*. "I try to live within that line between despondency and hope. I'm suited to walk that line, right between the fire. I see it as right straight down the middle of the line, really." The album did seem rife with life's harsher realities, with references to lost love, mortality, and a fallen world, but a world not void of a redeeming God. "It's not like, you know, Dante's *Inferno* or something. It doesn't paint a picture of goblins and goons and grotesque-looking creatures or anything like that," he later told Mikal Gilmore of *Rolling Stone*.

"I believe in a God of time and space, but if people ask me about that, my impulse is to point them back toward the songs. I believe in Hank Williams singing 'I Saw the Light.' I've seen the light, too."

—1997

Whatever the themes, the critics who "prophesied with their pens" eventually irked Dylan. He thought they were shortsighted in that they could only see the album as a reflection of Dylan's own mortality. "It's one thing that we all have in common, isn't it? But I didn't see any one critic say: 'It deals with *my* mortality'—you know, his *own*," remarked Dylan to Gilmore. "As if he's immune in some kind of way—like whoever's writing about the record has got eternal life and the singer doesn't."

1998

In January 1998, Stanford University played host to an international Bob Dylan conference. One of the speakers, Mark Gonnerman, a research fellow at Stanford's Center for Buddhist Studies, addressed Dylan's religious history during his cleverly titled presentation, "The Sound of One Dog Barking: Bob Dylan and Religious Experience." Gonnerman thought Dylan's treatment of religion during the 1979-1981 period was his least interesting. "Who knows?" he said of Dylan's encounter with Jesus. "Maybe all his questions were answered." Imre Salusinszky, for one, didn't expect such academic interest in Dylan's lyrics to continue. "The political climate in our universities," he wrote in *The Telegraph*, "hardly encourages the study of an artist who is a white, male, Zionist, Christian, American millionaire."[85]

Among the lyrics that academia would no doubt find the least interesting are those of "Gotta Serve Somebody," a song Dylan reintroduced to the stage on June 19, 1998, in Belfast, Northern Ireland. It just didn't leave listeners any wiggle room in the spiritual realm: A person is either serving the devil or the Lord. The song remained a show opener for the balance of the year.

While Dylan was busy touring Europe in the summer of 1998, the results of an industry poll were published in the twentieth anniversary issue of *Contemporary Christian Music* magazine, as determined by a panel of critics: Dylan's 1979 album, *Slow Train Coming*, was voted number seven of the Top 100 albums, and checking in at number six in the Top 10 songs was its opening track, "Gotta Serve Somebody." Although these results obviously show a critical awareness of Dylan's contribution to the "Christian music" field, it would seem that for most listeners of this genre, Dylan remains a relatively unknown figure.

One listener in the field, who is very familiar with Dylan and the *Slow Train Coming* album is Dallas Holm, the Christian singer who penned "Rise Again" (a song Dylan brought to the stage and the studio). When conducting songwriting workshops, Holm has been known to cite lyrics from *Slow Train Coming* and has recorded both "Gotta Serve Somebody" and "I Believe in You." "I think it's just an absolute monument of wonderful writing," he said of the album. "I mean, what was astounding to me is [Dylan] wrote things as a new Christian that some of us struggle for years to figure out how to say."[86]

Holm, who has been around since the infancy of what's now known as the "Contemporary Christian" music movement, says the field is lackluster now because many have forgotten their roots, not to mention their calling. "It's gotten increasingly more like the secular industry in that we've gotten very flavor-of-the-month oriented. There's a new artist every week and it's very much about image, dollars, and awards—all that stuff which is completely different from the time I started." The new breed of artists in contemporary Christian music circles (some of whom aren't familiar with Bob Dylan) might benefit from taking a peek into his back catalog.

Alex Ross, writing for *The New Yorker*, attended Dylan's concert on September 25, 1998, in Concord, California, a city where Dylan was anything but an unknown figure. "The crowd is dominated by ex- and neo-hippies from Berkeley, twenty miles to the west," observed Ross. "Dylan threatens to dampen their enthusiasm by opening with 'Gotta Serve Somebody,' the snarling gospel single with which he had horrified the counterculture in 1979."[87]

1999-2002

CHAPTER 8
Comfortable in his Own Skin

Audiences in early 1999 were no doubt pleasantly surprised that Dylan chose to include in his encore sets Buddy Holly's "Not Fade Away," a tribute to the singer Dylan had seen in concert forty years earlier in Duluth, Minnesota, just days before his death. But on February 2, an audience in Pensacola, Florida, may have been downright mystified when Dylan gave an onstage debut to a Christian hymn, Augustus Toplady's 1776 composition, "Rock of Ages."

What prompted Dylan to sing "Rock of Ages" is anyone's guess. Whatever the case, the folks in Pensacola heard Dylan sing about the same Rock—Jesus—he had sung about twenty years before. "Solid Rock" had carried the urgency of newborn zeal at that time; the "Rock of Ages" in 1999 sounded, and felt, much different. Although it was given a mellow country treatment—as opposed to the fiery, bristling delivery of an up-tempo "Solid Rock"—the reference to Jesus as the Savior was apparent. If Dylan still believed that the highest form of song is prayer, as he had said in 1976, then "Rock of Ages" amounted to a humble prayer offered up to the Most High.

A few weeks later, on February 23, in Buffalo, New York, Dylan brought another hymn to the stage; this time it was "Pass Me Not, O Gentle Savior," a composition originally penned by the noted nineteenth-century hymn writer Fanny Crosby. The next evening in Amherst, Massachusetts, Dylan sang Crosby's hymn again.

"The one that really surprises me," wrote award-winning author Alan Jacobs, "is 'Pass Me Not, O Gentle Savior,' which…absolutely reeks with evangelical spirituality: 'When on others thou art calling / Do not pass me by.' And the lyrics of the verses are based on the man who said to Jesus, 'Lord, I believe, help thou my unbelief.' I'm trying not to read Dylan's doing that song in autobiographical terms, but the temptation is hard to resist."[88]

When it was announced that Dylan would be joining Paul Simon, a fellow Jew, for a summer tour in 1999, *Time* magazine listed some pros and cons of their collaboration. Under the "pros," the magazine suggested that the two could bond over "failed projects"—Simon's *The Capeman* and Dylan's Christianity. But four shows into the tour, Dylan introduced "Hallelujah, I'm Ready to Go" to an audience in Vancouver, Canada. The traditional song, which became something of a staple during the tour, includes these lyrics: "Sinner don't wait / Before it's too late / He's a wonderful Savior to know / I fell on my knees / He answered my pleas

/ Hallelujah, I'm ready to go." So much for Dylan's "failed project"; the song was obviously in the same theological vein as "Rock of Ages" and "Pass Me Not, O Gentle Savior."

On June 14, Dylan played a solo gig in Eugene, Oregon, that included the live debut for "Down Along the Cove," a song off 1967's *John Wesley Harding*. That was the album that didn't jibe with the countercultural climate in which it was created. When he finished the song, Dylan told the crowd, "I want to say hello to all the ex-hippies tonight. I've never been a hippie myself, but…I'm an honorary hippie!"

Less than a month later, while in Maryland Heights, Missouri, Dylan introduced another traditional song to the stage; this time the show opener was "Somebody Touched Me." Like its predecessor, "Hallelujah, I'm Ready to Go," it received a number of outings during the tour. Its lyrics repeatedly speak of being touched by "the hand of the Lord"—reminiscent of Dylan's description of his encounter with Jesus. "Jesus put His hand on me," Dylan told journalist Karen Hughes in 1980. "It was a physical thing… I felt my whole body tremble. The glory of the Lord knocked me down and picked me up." In the same year, Dylan related his encounter in similar terms for journalist Paul Vitello: "Let's just say I had a knee-buckling experience."

In 1999, the singer was also telling jokes and one-liners from the stage, though *Rolling Stone* writer Mark Jacobson apparently was unaware of it. "Whatever his current theology, I, for one, would like to know what ever happened to the Jewish jokes in Bob Dylan," Jacobson wrote. "Maybe being born again beat the stand-up out of him, or maybe it was just the sheer weight of being Bob Dylan for so many years." Maybe, though, praising God through song and doling out corny jokes had proven to be a perfect anti-dote for "the sheer weight of being Bob Dylan"—an insightful phrase that true fans and Dylan-watchers can fully appreciate.

During a month-long touring break in August, Dylan helped fulfill a long-standing dream of Curtis Hanson, an award-winning film director (*L.A. Confidential*): Hanson had wanted to enlist the singer's help ever since the release of the 1973 film *Pat Garrett and Billy the Kid*, Dylan's last substantial soundtrack contribution. As Hanson was working on his current project, *Wonder Boys*, Dylan popped into the editing room and checked out some of the footage, subsequently writing "Things Have Changed" for the film. Its lyrics spoke of walking "forty miles of bad road" and maintained that "if the Bible is right, the world will explode"—familiar territory for Dylan the songwriter.

Not long after recording "Things Have Changed," Dylan hit the road again, surprising fans in West Palm Beach, Florida, with "The Heart That You Own," a Dwight Yoakam cover. But it was at his next concert, in Atlanta, where fans may very well have been freaked out when Dylan opened with "I Am the Man, Thomas," a song about the crucifixion and resurrection of Jesus that he would open many shows with in the years to come. Its first-person perspective and lyrical focus—Jesus addressing His doubting disci-ple—echoed Dallas Holm's "Rise Again," the song Dylan had per-formed in 1980-1981 and recorded in 1992.

"Here's my two cents' worth," said Ken Wilson, who heard Dylan's debut of "I Am the Man, Thomas" in Atlanta that night. "If I'd had a dramatic conversion to any religion and written songs espousing it, and preached about it in concert, and then later came to think of it as bunk, I'd have to swallow awfully hard before singing any of those songs again. And I sure wouldn't be covering—much less opening concerts with—other [people's] songs espousing that same delusive faith."

In October, the reigning poet laureate of the U.K., Andrew Motion, was interviewed on National Poetry Day. A longtime Dylan fan, Motion commented on what he liked about Dylan the artist: "The concentration and surprise of his lyrics, the beauty of his melodies and the rasp of his anger; the dramatic sympathy between the words and the music; the range of devotions; the power of self-renewal; his wit; his surrealism; the truth to his experience." Motion's favorite Dylan lyrics? Those of the 1966 classic, "Visions of Johanna."[89]

During the same month, Dylan appeared with his friend T-Bone Burnett in an episode of the situation comedy *Dharma and Greg* ("Play Lady Play"), in which Dharma auditioned for a band and engaged in some down-to-earth banter with Dylan. From being praised by a poet laureate on foreign shores, to opening his shows with songs about Jesus, to appearing on a television comedy show in his home country, Dylan seemed to be comfortable in his own skin.

On the heels of the summer tour with Paul Simon, a fall tour then cranked up with former Grateful Dead bass player Phil Lesh. On Halloween night in Chicago, after Phil Lesh and Friends had finished their set, another act took the stage before Dylan: comedian Steven Wright. This wasn't the first time the deadpan comic opened a concert for Dylan. Actor and comedian Bob Goldthwait told Joseph Sia of *On the Tracks* that Wright is so enamored with Dylan that he did several gigs in Los Angeles just so he could open for the singer. Shortly after the popular comedian exited the stage on this last Halloween of the twentieth century, Dylan opened yet another show with the narrative of Jesus in "I Am the Man, Thomas."

Dylan concluded his 1999 tour in Newark, Delaware. Before the night was out, the crowd heard the debut of the apocalyptic "This World Can't Stand Long," with its telling line: "This world's been destroyed before / Because it was too full of sin / For that very reason / It's going to be destroyed again / If only we give our hearts to God / Let Him lead us by the hand / Nothing in this world to fear / He'll lead you across the burning sand." The song's lyrical emphasis easily parallels the between-song bantering of a born-again Bob Dylan back in 1979-1981, though now it seemed clear that the singer was content to have some of his songs do the talking for him. The possibility of twenty-first century gospel lectures between songs at a Dylan concert seems remote, but few eyebrows should be raised if he continues to sing about Jesus, the Jesus who is apparently still vitally important to his life.

Author Larry Yudelson noted in *Moment* magazine that the Dylan family regularly gathered for Christmas, which he saw as significant. "Dylan grew up in a family that knew it was Jewish, but without much religion," he wrote. "That goes a long way to explain the early rootlessness of Dylan who has always in his lyrics had a very strong religious sense, from the early 'With God on Our Side' to 'All Along the Watchtower,' with its imagery from the Book of Isaiah."[90]

It would certainly be a difficult task to divorce Dylan's essence from biblical tradition. "Things Have Changed," was, according to Rob Sheffield of *Rolling Stone*, "one of those grim, intense Book of Deuteronomy howls he comes up with whenever he's in the mood to make all other rock & roll singers sound like scared kittens."

That's the thing with Bob Dylan. No other rock singer does what he does: raise support for an Orthodox Jewish ministry, sing about Jesus, mine the depths of American roots music, perform at a county fairground, a gambling casino, and a religious event before the pope. Or write lyrics that provoke academic treatment: In November 1999, at the National Communication Association's annual convention, panel members presented academic papers on Dylan's work: "Street-Legal: Dylan's Pre-Christian Period" (Jeff Shires); "Slow Train Coming: A Metaphorical Analysis" (Joseph Blaney); "A Simple Twist of Faith: Spiritual Ambiguity and Rhetorical Perspectivism in Bob Dylan's Infidels" (Brett Miller); and "Jokerman: Bob Dylan's Metaphors of Space, Time and Eternity" (Joe Munshaw). The event was sponsored by the Religious Communication Association, which is affiliated with the host organization.

By the end of 1999, Michael Gray's long-awaited book—*Song & Dance Man III: The Art of Bob Dylan*—was finally released. In the preface, Gray looked back over the period since 1981, when his previous volume had left off. "Dylan's latest album was *Saved* and he was touring with ugly musicians around stadiums of the resentful damned. He was about as hip as General Franco," wrote Gray, who also acknowledged Dylan's current attraction to younger audiences, those who "have in front of them the enviable pleasures of getting to know his vast back catalogue."

As for touring, Dylan was showing no signs of slowing down: In 1999, he played to 121 audiences, the most ever in his career—and that at the age of fifty-eight. In his updated book, Gray cited author Stephen Scobie, who once concluded that Dylan's songs from the 1970s alone would qualify him as the greatest songwriter of his time. Gray went a step further, asserting that Dylan's output from the 1980s and 1990s would still place him at the top of the songwriter heap.

The indomitable Clinton Heylin, the most prolific Dylan author, singled out Dylan's 1999 repertoire in his updated biography, *Bob Dylan: Behind the Shades Revisited.* "His recent performances suggest someone who longs to return to the simple embrace of his original Born Again faith. Of the dozen or so covers added to the repertoire in 1999, the likes of 'Hallelujah, I'm Ready to Go,' 'Somebody Touched Me,' 'Pass Me Not, O Gentle Savior,' 'I Am the Man, Thomas,' and 'Rock of Ages' testify to both a world-weary yearning for release and an abiding faith in Christ's promise of redemption," Heylin wrote. "The way that Dylan's 59-year-old vocal cords can still communicate the meaning of a song like 'Rock of Ages' suggests he continues to set his affections on things above, even if he has let other things get in the way of that love."[91]

But Dylan's choice of songs and the truth they express seem to prove just the opposite—that "other things" have not gotten in the way of that love. "So far as Dylan is concerned, the song is his, and he'll do with it as he likes," Sean Dolan wrote in *On the Tracks* about Dylan's choice of cover songs. "He treats it like one of his own: alive, sturdy, road-tested, durable, its existence alone sufficient testimony to its vitality and worthiness. Dylan's belief in these songs—in song—becomes a way of seeing, a way of understanding the world, of explaining it and human nature. They express eternal, universal truths, in the same way that the Bible might."[92]

Before 1999 came to a close, singer, lawyer, and environmental activist Peter Garrett touched on the subject of Dylan's faith at a monthly meeting at the St. James Anglican Church in Sydney, Australia. During a discussion on, of all things, ethics and biotechnology (airing on national radio via ABC), Garrett couldn't resist quoting a certain poet from Minnesota. "It was the singer/poet Bob Dylan who at one of his most outwardly religious stages, a stage of his career many people deplored as I recall, wrote, 'You've got to serve somebody.' And this was a very succinct statement of a central biblical theme," said Garrett. "But I think he was also pointing something else out at the same time, and that is, he was implying that you cannot live fully if the only thing that you're living for is yourself."

2000

On January 25, 2000, Dylan suffered the loss of his mother, who died in St. Paul, Minnesota, at the age of eighty-four. A private funeral service was reportedly held the following day in Duluth. Beatty Zimmerman's appearance at the Kennedy Center Honors in December 1997 and an interview she gave in June 1999 marked two rare moments when she briefly stepped into the glare of the public spotlight. By all accounts, she was a kind, modest, talkative, humorous woman who loved her family and friends.

In February, the *New York Times* reported on Natalie Cole's fiftieth birthday bash, at which the singer chatted about a gift Dylan had recently given her. Cole's sister, Carol, had urged her to record one of her favorite Dylan songs, "Gotta Serve Somebody." Cole, though, didn't know how to get around singing the last two highly personal verses (Dylan's self-referential "You may call me Zimmy..."). Her producer, Phil Ramone, contacted Dylan, who rewrote the last two verses especially for her. "Bob's own people were more surprised than we were. He had never, ever done that before," said Cole. Natalie Cole's version of "Gotta Serve Somebody" appears on her 1999 release, *Snowfall in the Sahara*.[105]

British soul singer Gabrielle wanted to borrow the music to another Dylan hit from the 1970s, "Knockin' on Heaven's Door." According to Brian Boyd of *The Irish Times*, after sending Dylan a demo of her song "Rise," he wrote back to her, expressing his appreciation for her song and giving her permission to use any portion of "Knockin' on Heaven's Door." This, too, was unusual. Dylan receives thousands of requests annually from musicians seeking permission to use his work; most requests are routinely rejected. The concession to Gabrielle marked another first for Dylan.

Less than two weeks into the first leg of Dylan's 2000 tour, he had included all five of the gospel songs he introduced the previous year. During the course of the year he would debut both old and new Dylan compositions, as well as some cover songs. "Tell Me That It Isn't True" and "Country Pie," two songs off 1969's *Nashville Skyline*, saw the light of day, and "If Dogs Run Free" from 1970's *New Morning* also became a part of the set lists. Original songs from the 1990s also were aired: "10,000 Men," "Standing in the Doorway," and "Things Have Changed." He performed "Searching for a Soldier's Grave" numerous times, along with a one-time performance of "Blue Bonnet Girl." Dylan continued pulling out surprises for those who closely followed his road show.

In an interview in April 2000 on the Internet, The Who's Pete Townshend was asked, "Seeing as how you've influenced so many musicians in your career, whom would you label as your number one musical influence?" "Bob Dylan," said Townshend. "He told me, I'm paraphrasing, that a folk singer is simply a man with a very good memory. I very much appreciate his memory. But I also appreciate his courage and invention."[93]

Dylan's influence in Europe could also be seen on May 15, 2000, when he picked up the Swedish Polar Music Prize in Stockholm along with fellow honoree violinist Isaac Stern. The awards were presented to Dylan and Stern by King Carl Gustaf XVI of Sweden.

The following month, a less formal accolade was bestowed upon Dylan. He just barely landed a slot on an Internet list, "The Kosher Top 10 Pop and Rock Stars." (David Lee Roth of Van Halen was number one; Dylan came in at number ten). "Should be higher up because he made such classics as 'Like a Rolling Stone' and 'Blowin' in the Wind,'" wrote one critic, "but as a dabbler in Christianity he slides down the list."[94]

In June, as Dylan joined another tour, Phil Lesh and Friends, the Grateful Dead's former bass player spoke to a journalist about the Dylan connection: "The second song I ever learned with [the Grateful Dead] was Dylan's 'Love Minus Zero/No Limit,'" Lesh told Chris Macias of the *Sacramento Bee*. "It's been traditional for [the Grateful Dead] to interpret Dylan's songs. We felt like we brought something to the table in the interpretation of his material. Plus, Jerry [Garcia] and Bob had a very tight relationship, even though they probably didn't see each other that often. They were kindred souls in a concrete way."

By the end of June 26, 2000, even prime-time television viewers weren't immune to Dylan's influence. Sixteen million viewers in America tuned into the two-hour special "Search for Jesus," hosted by ABC News anchor Peter Jennings. A clip from Dylan's song "When You Gonna Wake Up?" played in the background as John the Baptist's ministry of repentance was being described.

In August, the A&E television network aired a two-hour biography special on Dylan. After dealing with the 1979-1981 era for a few minutes, narrator Harry Smith said, "By 1982, it appeared that Dylan had changed yet again and moved away from an overt

Christian theology…Ultimately, questions about Dylan's faith
faded away unanswered as his music returned to less religious
concerns." Just weeks after the A&E broadcast, Dylan could
be found on stages in Europe opening his concerts with "I Am the
Man, Thomas," "Hallelujah, I'm Ready to Go," and "Somebody
Touched Me," all glowing examples of an "overt Christian
theology."

The October 2000 issue of Q, a music magazine published in
England, was wholly devoted to Dylan and included a foreword
from U2's lead singer: "In your twenties you're more interested
in 'The Times They Are A-Changin,'" said Bono. "But Bob Dylan's
got you from the cradle to the grave. For instance, I loved *Slow
Train Coming*. I even loved *Saved*. People thought *Saved* was his
bumper-sticker-Christianity album, but for me it sounds like a real
cry for help."

2001

To kick off a banner year for awards, 2001 started with Dylan
receiving a Golden Globe in the Best Original Song/Motion
Picture category for "Things Have Changed," beating out some
formidable competition from Garth Brooks and Sting. On being
announced the winner at the January 21 show, Dylan exhibited a
"priceless look of surprise," as one newspaper put it, then took to
the stage and kept his acceptance speech short and sweet: "This is
quite something, really. Thanks Hollywood Foreign Press, thanks
to my band, record company and everyone in my family." Next up
was actress Julia Roberts, who was to present the Best Director

award. "Never thought I'd follow Bob Dylan in my life," she quipped.

As is often the case, the Golden Globes foreshadowed some of the Oscar winners at the Academy Awards. On March 25, Dylan received his first Oscar, also for "Things Have Changed," which he performed live via satellite feed from Australia, where he was touring. A few weeks before the performance, some people were surprised by the content of a press release Dylan issued: "It's quite an honor to be nominated and, if circumstances permitted, I'd no doubt be there. We'll be touring Australia at that time, however, and it would mean canceling shows that had been planned some time ago. So, while it's impossible for me to appear on the Academy Awards in person, I'd be thrilled to perform live via satellite, if that could be arranged. That way, I wouldn't be disappointing my fans in Australia and I'd still be able to accept the Academy's gracious offer. I really hope it all works out."

Some wondered if these words had been written on Dylan's behalf, but after his Oscar was announced, there was no doubt whose words these were as a large video screen beamed his image from Sydney: "And I want to thank the Academy who were bold enough to give me this award for this song," said a genuinely surprised Dylan, "which obviously...is a song which doesn't pussyfoot around or turn a blind eye to human nature. And God bless you all with peace, tranquility, and goodwill. Thanks."

Prior to Dylan's Australian tour, a few faith-related snippets appeared in an Australian newspaper, *The Age*. "I took a sabbatical from Bob during his Christian era," said film producer Bob Weiss.

James Griffin, a singer/songwriter and producer of ABC-TV's *The Last Word* who opened for Dylan in 1986, found it difficult to comprehend Dylan's spiritual journey: "I struggled with the conversions to Christianity and back to Judaism," said Griffin. "I'm not personally attracted to hymns, although '[Gotta] Serve Somebody' is a terrific song."

But Ian Lovell, a fifties and sixties retro retailer and former manager of the Australian pop group Goanna, dug beneath the surface: "*Slow Train Coming*, the first evangelical album, polarized everyone. They forgot that blues is a child of gospel and work songs, and we adored the three gospel albums," said Lovell. "That period when there was a division between those who loved it and others who thought Bob had lost the plot reminded me of being back in boarding school. I can't remember a time when my interest in Bob has diminished."[95]

In March, Columbia released an official live album, the Japanese import *Bob Dylan Live: 1961-2000*, which began with "Somebody Touched Me," a traditional gospel song. It was followed by a forty-year-old recording of Dylan singing another traditional song, "Wade in the Water," which spoke of God "troubling" the waters that the children of Israel, led by Moses, would be passing through.

"Best of all, the album starts with a forthright declaration of faith, featuring the classic 'Somebody Touched Me,'" noted David Dawes of *Canadian Christianity*. "There are several other Bible-based songs, including 'Wade in the Water,' 'Dead Man, Dead Man,' and 'Slow Train.'"[113] The compilation of live offerings was capped off by the recent award-winning "Things Have Changed."

As Dylan's sixtieth birthday approached, there would be the predictable onslaught of articles summing up his forty years as an artist. Most writers referred to the "Christian period" as a passing phase. In the middle of it all, a press release issued on May 17, 2001, indicated that Dylan had agreed to participate on a track for the forthcoming tribute album, *Pressing On: The Gospel Songs of Bob Dylan*. Considering that the project only featured songs from *Slow Train Coming* and *Saved*, his participation would have seemed odd if he no longer believed in Jesus as the Messiah. After all, these were the very albums that had ruffled so many feathers with their overt sentiments about Jesus, judgment, and redemption.

Reacting to a new Dylan biography by Howard Sounes, critic Steve Turner of *Christianity Today* wrote that the author connects Dylan's conversion with "an earlier belief (not uncommon among rock stars) that his songs came from God. 'It was a small step, apparently,' he concludes, 'from this to flinging himself headfirst into orthodox religion.'"

For Turner, this angle didn't seem to fit. "But Dylan's conversion appeared to be a genuine work of regeneration rather than a chase for the source of creativity. He studied the Bible in depth, put his career on the line (for a time) by refusing to play his back catalog in concert, alienated his friends by accusing them of spiritual blindness, and horrified his record company by recording songs of a Christian explicitness unparalleled in the rock genre."[96]

A number of prominent artists were asked by *Rolling Stone* to comment on Dylan's sixtieth birthday. "He's a cyclical person, as all great artists are—he sort of comes and goes," said Don Henley of the Eagles. "And he's not afraid to go off on tangents—the Christianity thing, for instance. But at the same time, I think 'Gotta Serve Somebody' is a great song."

Author Camille Paglia remarked that the essence of Dylan's roots was "a total product of the Jewish culture, where the word is sacred." Singer/songwriter Lucinda Williams thought Dylan to be a good example in terms of "sticking to his guns artistically and still going out there and rocking."

Bono thought Dylan's words always had "an almost biblical uprightness… Bob is like religion: He'll get you one way or the other! I'm sure he has his demons—the records pay tribute to that. But he's still alive and doing his best work."

Confirming Bono's sentiments, it seemed, was an article in the *Jewish Journal* of Los Angeles: "His religious identity has always been a source of mystery (and obsession) to Jewish fans. He flirted with Christian messianism, sent his children to a Beverly Hills Hebrew school, nearly joined a kibbutz and danced with the Lubavitchers. A generation that looked to Dylan for The Way seemed forever disappointed that he was often lost himself." He may well have been lost, but Dylan certainly claimed he had been found in 1979 and continues to point to the One that the Jewish writers of the New Testament refer to as "The Way, the Truth and the Life."

COMFORTABLE IN HIS OWN SKIN

Meticulous observers noted that a number of artists who happened to be performing on Dylan's sixtieth birthday paid tribute to him: In Santa Barbara, California, Tom Petty and the Heartbreakers included "Knockin' on Heaven's Door" in their encore; U2 included "Forever Young" in an encore for their audience in Toronto; and at a separate concert in Toronto, Gordon Lightfoot mentioned that he was two and a half years older than Dylan before paying tribute to him by singing the biblically rich "Ring Them Bells."

Beginning on Dylan's birthday and running for four days was "The Never-Ending Birthday," a festival in Alba, Italy, where more than fifty musicians covered Dylan's songs at two venues. Musicians included bluesmen, songwriters, jazz bands, cover bands, and even a forty-piece band. Photo exhibits, video presentations and roundtable discussions were also featured at the festival, designed to "spread Dylan's poetics." Other musical tributes were held overseas in Turkey and England, as well as in Dylan's birthplace, Duluth, Minnesota.

Politicians even got into the act. Mike Briggs, a Republican from Fresno, California, played a tape of Dylan's "Forever Young" and urged his colleagues from the state assembly to join in for a sing-along. "The 79 other lawmakers stared at him. Finally, about 18 lined up and belted out the song," noted the Associated Press. The Assembly unanimously approved Briggs' resolution to congratulate Dylan on his birthday and called him "one of the great influences on modern American music." Virginia Strom-Martin, a Democrat from Duncan Mills, confessed that she became a "rabid Bob Dylan fan" in 1965 when her high school English teacher

introduced her to 'The Times They Are A-Changin.'" But Russ
Bogh, a Republican from Yucaipa, paused and innocently
inquired, "On behalf of the thirty-something caucus, who exactly
is this Bob Dylan guy?"

When asked on a BBC news show what Bob Dylan, at age sixty,
had to offer, sixties singer Donovan, who appeared with Dylan in
the 1965 documentary *Dont Look Back*, replied, "An edge to disturb complacent hearts." In a birthday tribute in Canada's *The
Globe and Mail*, Heather Mallick pointed out that Dylan "was one
of the first rock stars to become a born-again Christian and mean
it, staying with it for years after it emptied his concerts and deci-
mated his record sales."

Over time Dylan's concerts began to fill back up, but the evidence
for decimation of record sales is compelling. Until the much-publicized "comeback" of *Time Out of Mind* (1997), the post-*Slow
Train Coming* years were marked by a stunning lack of commercial
success. The following studio albums from Dylan had not
achieved the minimum gold status of 500,000 units sold, as of
October of 2000: *Saved, Shot of Love, Empire Burlesque, Knocked Out
Loaded, Down in the Groove, Oh Mercy, Under the Red Sky, Good As I
Been to You*, and *World Gone Wrong. Infidels*, released in 1983, was
the only exception, and its commercial success may have been
attributed to early reports that its songs reflected a reversal of
Dylan's Bible-thumping furor.

Dylan's releases from 1980-1993 weren't exactly akin to the cal-
iber of *Highway 61 Revisited*, although some are receiving greater
appreciation with the passage of time. But a legitimate argument

can be made that Dylan's record sales did take a dive because of the fallout brought on by his encounter with Jesus; every single Dylan studio album released prior to 1980 had gone gold, platinum, or multi-platinum.

Looking back, a journalist for *The Globe and Mail* saw the born-again Christian reality as "really bizarre." Peter Shard of *The Age* saw a "musical fall from grace in the religion-obsessed *Slow Train Coming, Saved*, and *Shot of Love*."[119] And Anthony DeCurtis of *Rolling Stone* went a step further, viewing the 1979-1981 period as the "born-again scourge of God."

After maintaining that *Slow Train Coming* "consigned nonbelievers to Hell in no uncertain terms," Brian Doherty of *Reason* magazine saw things change after "Gotta Serve Somebody" earned a Grammy. "Once the novelty wore off, his relentless preaching murdered his commercial prospects for over a decade," writes Doherty. "As [biographer Howard] Sounes accurately notes, 'Electricity had annoyed folk purists, but religion bothered everybody.'"[97]

However, the "religion" didn't literally bother everybody. *Slow Train Coming* was "a breakthrough," according to U2's Bono. "I was always annoyed that rock could cover any taboo—sexual, cultural, political. That was part of its energy," he told Edna Gundersen of *USA Today*. "But nobody could be upfront about their spiritual life, unless it was the exotic sort. No white people could sing about God, that was certain, before Bob Dylan. He opened me to those possibilities."[98]

As for Dylan's *Saved* album, Green Day's Billie Joe Armstrong wasn't about to poke fun at the effort: "Even as a Jesus freak, he was trying to challenge himself and go with his instincts," Armstrong told Gundersen. "It's so human. He's seen as such a legend that people forget his human qualities."

"Jews still wince at the memory of his forays into gospel music (although Leonard Cohen has rightly observed that those songs are quite the best ever written in the genre)," observed David Vest. "As for Christian fans, they still scramble for the merest hint that Dylan might actually share their dogma."[99]

As J.J. Goldberg noted in *Forward* magazine, Jewish fans have also done some scrambling of their own: "Over the years, a cottage industry grew up to ferret out Judaic content—some genuine, some merely imagined—in his lyrics," writes Goldberg. "Fans stalked him on his spiritual journeys the way other performers might be staked out during restaurant outings. Jewish Dylanophiles raged when he publicly dabbled in Christianity around 1980, then exulted when he flirted with Lubavitch chasidism a few years later. Throughout, Dylan seemed to become more and more desperate to preserve his privacy."[100]

Fortunately for Dylan, he seems to have been largely successful in preserving the privacy of his family life. However, biographer Howard Sounes was the one who let the world know that Dylan had a daughter in 1986 with singer Carolyn Dennis. The couple married the same year but divorced by 1992. Dennis had toured occasionally with Dylan and contributed vocals to a number of his albums over the course of a decade—*Street-Legal, Slow Train*

Coming, Shot of Love, Empire Burlesque, Knocked Out Loaded, and *Down in the Groove.*

In 1992, readers of *Follow Your Dream International,* a Bruce Springsteen fanzine, learned how Dennis and Dylan first met. "I went on the road for a couple of weeks with Burt Bacharach doing a tour in South America, and I came back to a surprising phone call from a girl who was dating Mr. Dylan at the time," said Dennis. "I have to say—as embarrassing as it might be—I didn't know who he was, because my young life had been so reclusive and so sheltered. So I called and I asked, 'Who is Bob Dylan? I got a call, they want me to come and audition for this guy named Bob Dylan. Who is he?' And the union went, 'What? Oh my God! In the sixties there was nobody but Bob Dylan and the Beatles!' It was May 1978 when I first met him and started working for him, did the U.S. [tour], and started recording with him."

Dennis also described how she helped Dylan select his other singers: "He knew that I'd basically bring in what he was after, people that could go after a feeling; that it wasn't so much standing there with the music and trying to prove how perfectly you could sing, but people who had a story in their voices; when they'd sing there was a feeling there," she said. "That feeling comes from life experiences, and that's what he was after. He wanted his show to have that kind of spontaneous spiritual type of feeling to it."[101]

In 2001, Christopher Farley of *Time* magazine asked Dylan why he concealed his second marriage. "It's not private to me," said Dylan, adding, "She is a fantastic singer. She's a gospel singer mainly. One of her uncles was Blind Willie Johnson. What more do you need to know about somebody?"

Mikal Gilmore of *Rolling Stone* asked Dylan if he felt resentful toward biographers who pried into his life. "I don't feel that way at all," he said. "At the same time, there's a person that writes these kinds of books that has what they call a poetical lack of self. I think it's more of an elitist thing to write about me and have other people read about me. I mean, what is there to expose? We all belong to the human race, I assume. Am I that uncommon? But I don't think that anything's even come close to the truth."

Some of Dylan's most intriguing public comments came a couple of months after his birthday, while he was on his usual summer tour of Europe. At a press conference in Rome, one journalist asked if he thought there was a "religious feeling amongst your hardcore fans." Dylan replied, "And then what religion are they? I mean what sacrifices do they make…and to whom do they sacrifice, these hardcore fans? If they do sacrifice then okay, we've got hardcore religious fans. And I'd like to know when and where they make their sacrifices, because I'd like to be there."[102]

Comments like these, humorous but also thoughtful and deadly serious, make Dylan an intriguing interview. Someone else asked if he looked for comfort in religion. "I try," he said. "Who would I be if I didn't try?"

Back in the U.S., anticipating Dylan's upcoming concert near Tempe, Arizona, journalist Gilbert Garcia reflected on his infamous 1979 concerts in Tempe, where audiences were hostile to his gospel presentation. The subtitle to Garcia's article—"Bob Dylan's career has only begun to recover from a slump that started 22 years ago in Tempe"—might sound a bit dramatic, but the article presented a number of persuasive arguments. Referring to Dylan's renewed popularity since 1997's *Time Out of Mind*, Garcia writes: "What's strange about this latent burst of Bob love is that it followed nearly two solid decades in pop-culture purgatory for Dylan, a period ushered in by his late '70s transformation into a born-again Christian. Throughout the '80s, and for much of the '90s, Dylan was routinely dismissed as a cranky, croaky-throated has-been."

Garcia says the Tempe shows marked a turning point for Dylan when his commercial standing and creative confidence began a downward spiral. He failed to see any single make it to the top forty, and his albums wouldn't reach the top ten until nearly eighteen years later. "More important, he would never completely shake the feeling of distance and distrust with his audience that those shows created," Garcia said. The world was ready to embrace Bob Dylan again. The question was whether Dylan was willing to open himself to them.

Edna Gundersen, the journalist from *USA Today* who has interviewed Dylan frequently over the last fifteen years, spoke with him just prior to the release of his new collection of songs, *"Love and Theft."* Published on September 10, 2001, Gundersen's article noted how the opening track, "Tweedle Dee and Tweedle Dum," conveyed "the nature of wickedness in modern times."

"I feel an obligation to play the best songs," he told her. "As I look through my repertoire, I don't really see a lot of bad songs. I couldn't sing them if there wasn't something profound in them." He also spoke about some common misconceptions in his own compositions. "People focus on the senators and congressmen in 'The Times They Are A-Changin',' but never the Nietzschean aspects. The spirit of 'God is dead' was in the air, but Nietzsche was the son of a bourgeois pastor. That turns the rationale on its head." And when asked how he saw his future, he simply replied—in typical Dylanesque fashion—"I don't."

On September 11, 2001, Dylan's album *"Love and Theft"* was released. On the heels of the tragedy in New York, Washington, and Pennsylvania, Richard Gehr of the *Village Voice* wrote: "The album, at least the way I hear it this week, is riddled with images of hopelessness, futility, apocalypse and revelation." After polling more than 600 music critics from the United States, the *Village Voice* ranked *"Love and Theft"* as number one—and this despite the fact that a good number of the critics were half Dylan's age. Among the voters was someone almost one-third Dylan's age, twenty-two-year-old Christian Hoard, a freelance journalist in New York. "Hoard included Dylan's disc on his ballot," wrote Geoff Boucher of the *Los Angeles Times*, "along with far younger artists Jay-Z and the White Stripes, but says Dylan is not the norm among classic rock figures. 'I don't listen to a lot of people in Dylan's age bracket. They're talking about things I don't necessarily relate to and drawing on styles I'm probably not terribly interested in.'"

Critics at *Rolling Stone* gave Dylan's new collection of songs the "Album of the Year" honor, after dishing out the first five-star album rating since a 1992 release by R.E.M. The granddaddy of rock and roll magazines also voted him "Artist of the Year."

Robert Hilburn of the *Los Angeles Times*, who, like Edna Gundersen, has been given unparalleled access to Dylan in recent years, sat down with Dylan just days after the September 11 horror. At one point, he asked Dylan to name one of his songs that had been widely misinterpreted. "Take 'Masters of War.' Every time I sing it, someone writes that it's an anti-war song," replied Dylan. "But there's no anti-war sentiment in that song. I'm not a pacifist. I don't think I've ever been one. If you look closely at the song, it's about what Eisenhower was saying about the dangers of the military-industrial complex in this country. I believe strongly in everyone's right to defend themselves by every means necessary."

When asked about the spirit of the 1950s and 1960s, Dylan said he knew it to be an unsettled, restless spirit but was reluctant to comment on the spirit of today, saying he was not "a forecaster of the times." However, he did sound a warning that if the U.S. wasn't careful, the country would wind up a multinational, multiethnic police state. "Not that America can't reverse itself," said Dylan. "Whoever invented America were the greatest minds we've ever seen, and [people] who understand what the Declaration of Independence and the Bill of Rights are all about will come to the forefront sooner or later."

Hilburn asked Dylan what it was like to be alternately adored and booed, specifically citing the boos that accompanied some of the gospel shows of 1979-1980. "I was booed at Newport before that," Dylan reminded him. "You can't worry about things like that. Miles Davis has been booed. Hank Williams was booed. Stravinsky was booed. You're nobody if you don't get booed sometime."

Does getting booed cause musicians to ease up or dig in? That depends on what type of artist you are, Dylan said, and he listed three types: superficial, natural, and supernatural. According to Dylan, superficial artists shouldn't even be onstage, because they have nothing to tell you; natural artists take the talent they have and use it to the best of their abilities. But supernatural artists go deeper, and the "deeper they go, the more buried gods they'll find." Hilburn naturally wondered how Dylan would describe himself. After laughing and saying his criteria should apply to other artists, he admitted that he didn't know where he'd fit, but that he could be called all three. But his noncommittal answer soon caved in to a deeper conviction. "I always felt," Dylan said, "that if I'm going to do anything in life, I want to go as deep as I can."[103]

Around the same time as the Hilburn interview, Christopher John Farley of *Time* magazine also interviewed Dylan. "I've had a God-given sense of destiny," said Dylan, speaking of his songwriting and performing. Earlier Dylan had told Edna Gundersen, "From the start, I had an extreme sense of destiny." And at the press conference in Rome, he expressed a similar sentiment. "I didn't really choose to do what you see me doing. I was chosen for it. If someone had consulted me, I would have preferred to be a scientist, a doctor, or an engineer. They are people I really admire. I don't admire people in the entertainment field."

On September 25, Dylan sat down with Mikal Gilmore of *Rolling Stone* for his final interview in support of *"Love and Theft."* Gilmore had previously interviewed Dylan in 1985 and 1986 and was curious about some of the events that had transpired since.

When he mentioned the 1991 Grammy show, at which Dylan had received his Lifetime Achievement Award, Gilmore discovered that the event had caused Dylan to become disillusioned with the music business. Several artists had agreed to perform on his behalf, but then backed out for one reason or another. "There's a few that are decent and God-fearing and will stand up in a righteous way," Dylan said. "But I wouldn't want to count on most of them."

As for *"Love and Theft,"* Dylan said the songs dealt with power, wealth, knowledge, and salvation. "If it's a great album," he told Gilmore, "it's a great album because it deals with great themes. The whole album deals with power. If life teaches us anything, it's that there's nothing that men and women won't do to get power." His intention had been to create a work that would "speak across the ages." "Career, by the way, isn't how I look at what I do," Dylan confessed to Gilmore. "Career is a French word. It means 'carrier.' It's something that takes you from one place to the other. I don't feel like what I do qualifies to be called a career. It's more of a calling."

When asked for his reaction to the events of September 11, Dylan quoted the Rudyard Kipling poem "Gentlemen-Rankers": "One of those Rudyard Kipling poems, 'Gentlemen-Rankers,' comes to my mind: 'We have done with Hope and Honour, we are lost to Love and Truth / We are dropping down the ladder rung by rung / And the measure of our torment is the measure of our youth / God help us, for we knew the worst too young!'

"If anything, my mind would go to young people at a time like this," said Dylan. "That's really the only way to put it...It is time now for great men to come forward. With small men, no great thing can be accomplished at the moment," said Dylan. He expressed confidence that the "people in charge"—presumably the Bush administration—had read the sixth century book *The Art of War* by Sun-Tzu. He quoted from the book: "If you know the enemy and know yourself, you need not fear the result of a hundred battles. If you know yourself and not your enemy, for every victory gained you will suffer a defeat. And he goes on to say, 'If you know neither the enemy nor yourself, you will succumb in every battle.'"

"Whoever's in charge, I'm sure they would have read that," said Dylan. "Things will have to change. And one of these things that will have to change: People will have to change their internal world."[104]

According to Merav Tassa, a writer for the *Jewish Journal* of Los Angeles, not long after the rounds of interviews, Dylan celebrated one of the most sacred days on the Jewish calendar, Yom Kippur, at Chabad of Encino.

At the end of October, as Dylan passed through Chicago for a concert, he spent some time with Dave Hoekstra, a journalist for the *Chicago Sun-Times*, for an article about a TV documentary on the Staple Singers. Dylan arrived on time and alone, wearing a black riverboat gambler outfit, a black cowboy hat, and black boots. "Like a schoolboy, Dylan tiptoed into the room with a shy stride," Hoekstra said, adding that Dylan and Mavis Staples exchanged gifts: a single red rose for her; a Beanie Baby bear, with hands upraised in prayer, for him. "As Mavis handed the yellow and tan bear to Dylan, she said, 'This is called 'Hope!' Dylan cradled the Beanie Baby, smiled and said, 'Of course.' He was touched."[105]

Although Dylan had tipped off some journalists at his summer press conference in Rome, the official news came down the pipeline in the fall: Reuters announced that Dylan would write a multi-volume autobiography. According to Dylan spokesman Elliot Mintz, the singer's decision was not to be taken as a response to a rash of recent unauthorized biographies. "He's lived a long, eventful life," said Mintz. "He's just elected to do this now."

2002

In early 2002, Dylan began touring the South. On February 5, when he stepped onstage before a crowd in Jacksonville, Florida, he opened with "Hallelujah, I'm Ready to Go," a song that reminded sinners of a "wonderful Savior to know." Next up was "The Times They Are A-Changin.'" Indeed, much had changed since Dylan wrote the latter composition in 1963, yet the same man was singing both of these testaments to truth, all in the glare of the spotlight and before thousands of fans.

The next evening in Charleston, South Carolina, Dylan opened with "I Am the Man, Thomas," the song about Jesus' crucifixion and resurrection. He then followed with his personalized anthem, "It Ain't Me, Babe," seemingly pointing up the significance of his opening song. Had Dylan's recent penchant for "I Am the Man, Thomas" reflected accurately on the identification of the long-awaited Messiah? In the song, Jesus repeatedly lets Thomas, his Jewish disciple, know "I Am the Man," as if the repetition is driving home a reality that relegates all doubt to dust.

In the biblical account, Thomas refused to believe unless he could see the nail-scarred hands of Jesus and put his fingers where the nails once were. A week after the request, Jesus granted a startled Thomas his wish and then uttered these words, which have echoed down the centuries: "Because you have seen me, you have believed; blessed are those who have not seen and yet have believed" (John 20:29 NIV).

Like millions of people in the ensuing generations, Bob Dylan was not an eyewitness to the risen Jesus walking around. But Dylan chose to believe, and if what Jesus says is true, then he is blessed because of it. According to the Mishna, a collection of oral laws compiled around 200 C.E. that forms the basic part of the Talmud, a person becomes an elder at age sixty. Was Dylan passing off some elderly wisdom through "I Am the Man, Thomas" and other songs about Jesus?

Even with all the focus on the diverse musical styles of Dylan's Grammy-nominated *Love and Theft*, the album's closing, blues-drenched song, "Sugar Baby," includes another biblical admonition: "Look up, look up / Seek your Maker / Before Gabriel blows his horn."

In the Bible the angel Gabriel makes only four appearances: twice in the book of Daniel, where details of the end of time are revealed to the Jewish prophet through a vision; and twice in the book of Luke, when two pregnant Jewish women receive an angelic visit and discover just who it is they are carrying to term—John the Baptist and Jesus the Messiah.

If Bob Dylan had indeed renounced Jesus or wanted to distance himself from his experience of 1979, then why did he participate in *Pressing On: The Gospel Songs of Bob Dylan*, a compilation featuring songs from *Slow Train Coming* and *Saved*? On the recording, Dylan, with his longtime friend, gospel singer Mavis Staples, sings a rewritten version of his 1979 composition, "Gonna Change My Way of Thinking."

And when Dylan included "Solid Rock" in the the first set list of his European spring tour of 2002, there were likely some more astonished folks at the Globe Arena in Stockholm, Sweden. He hadn't played the song since 1981. It's a song that presents some rather straightforward theology: "For me He was chastised / For me He was hated / For me He was rejected / In a world that He created...Nations are angry / Cursed are some / People are expecting a false peace to come / But I'm hanging on / To that solid rock / Made before the foundation of the world."[106] These are not the words and sentiments of a man who has forsaken belief in Jesus. He continued to sing it on a number of occasions throughout the tour.

When his new drummer, George Receli, had to return to the States because of an injury, old friend Jim Keltner was flown in as a replacement. Keltner had been the drummer during the gospel tours of 1979-1981 and had recently collaborated with Dylan on the Grammy-Award-winning *Time Out of Mind* from 1997. Now the two reunited and were offering "I Believe in You" and "Solid Rock" to crowds once again.

When Dylan introduced "Rock of Ages" into his concert repertoire in early 1999, few wondered if he was referring to the same rock of his "Solid Rock" of 1979-1981. Now, it's rather obvious. Journalist David Dawes recently remarked, "Surely, we can assume that Bob Dylan has enough money that he can afford not to sing things he doesn't believe."

EPILOGUE

Without question, Dylan's upbringing, particularly his Jewish heritage, has significantly shaped who he is today. Even nonreligious or nominally religious Jewish parents can't help but pass on to their children a rich spiritual and cultural history simply by virtue of their ethnic identity. Dylan's family life was similar to that of many Jewish households in America, in which Judaism is just enough of a factor to be an influence but not enough to become an obsession.

And clearly, late-night radio was largely responsible for shaping Dylan's life as a musician, poet, and spiritual seeker. The rhythms of the music, the cadence of the words, the passion of the stories all coalesced into a brilliant mind and soul centered on the spiritual nature of every aspect of life.

Beyond that, it's anyone's guess as to what other factors made Bob Dylan the man he is today—which, in essence, is the same man he has always been. The early influences that created in him an independent nature and the determination to live an authentic life are a part of the mystery that is Bob Dylan. Like few other entertainers, Dylan has resisted—or perhaps more accurately, completely ignored—all the pointless efforts his record company, fans, and critics have made to get him to conform to their image of who he should be. Over a period of forty years in the spotlight, Dylan has remained faithful to who he is and what he believes to be true.

For years, what many of his fans wanted him to be was their god. If a courtroom sketch artist had been forced to come up with a likeness of the counterculture's quintessential idol, the resulting composite image would have eerily resembled Bob Dylan. He looked and acted and thought the way they imagined their idol should. He appeared to be the leader they needed to revolutionize American society and usher in a world of peace and love and justice and equality. If anyone could reign over the unruly realm of hippiedom, the thinking went, it was Dylan.

What they didn't realize was that Dylan's primary concern was being true to himself, which was not the same thing as being true to anyone else's image of him. He refused to take on the title of prophet or idol or leader. His restless nature refused to be confined. And he continued his pilgrimage, never fearing where the search would take him. His pursuit was that of a curious, wandering, ever-questioning spiritual seeker, and the journey he was on led him straight to that most unpopular spot, the foot of the cross.

In fact, Dylan said during a concert in Omaha, Nebraska in 1980, "Years ago they used to say I was a prophet. I'd say, ... 'No, it's not me.' They used to convince me I was a prophet. Now, I come out and say, Jesus is the answer. They say, 'Bob Dylan? He's no prophet.' They just can't handle that." Those who admonished others to have an open mind closed their own minds to the words of their one-time prophet once it became evident that he really had embraced the things of God. They obviously did not want Dylan to remain true to what he believed if it meant that his beliefs would clash with theirs. Never before or since has the chasm between Dylan and his fans been as wide as it was in the first few years after he professed his faith in Jesus as the Messiah, the promised one of God. He had bought the whole deal: Jesus Christ, the Son of God, conceived by the Holy Spirit, born of the Virgin Mary, the one who suffered under Pontius Pilate, was cruci-fied, died, and was buried, descending to the dead only to rise again and ascend to heaven, where He is seated at the right hand of the Father until He comes again to judge humankind. That's it; that's the scenario that Dylan understood to represent truth, life-changing truth. He bought the entire gospel message.

Did that mean Dylan had turned his back on his Jewish roots, as so many claimed at the time? Clearly, he had not—and would not. Those who believe in God's direct involvement in the lives of individuals could not help but see God's hand in leading Dylan directly to the very people who would be in the best position to walk him through the transition from Jew to Messianic Jew. For this particular seeker, the walk was evidently not a very long one, since he had come to respect the person of Jesus long before 1979. Taking that walk with him was a gentile whose life was and still is inextricably linked with the people of Israel—Larry Myers, one of the Vineyard pastors who patiently answered Dylan's many questions about the Hebrew and Christian Scriptures.

"I have not been in the middle of anything quite like this before or since," Myers said of the electrically charged atmosphere at the Warfield Theater in 1979 when Dylan first came "out" as a Christian in concert. "Here was a man who was so highly revered, whose gifting and charisma were so strong, that many in those audiences would be forever changed by what they were seeing and hearing. What a profound honor and responsibility Bob and others like him have."[107]

"I know, from being out there with him, and talking with certain people, that a lot of people's lives were changed forever," echoed Jim Keltner, Dylan's drummer for the gospel tours. "In the Christian world, they say 'saved.' I know for a fact that happened to a lot of people."[108]

Regina Havis, one of Dylan's singers, was also there every step of the way during the tours of 1979-1981. She confirmed Keltner's account about peoples' lives being changed forever. "Some people that were there [at the concerts] came in high, ready to just rock 'n' roll, and they ended up being saved," remembered Havis, adding that she's convinced that Dylan "was sent to shed light on God's Word and how simple it is."[109]

Like others who have been "forever changed," Dylan and Larry Myers both take their responsibility seriously—each in their own way. For Bob Dylan, part of what that means is remaining true to what he believes in the songs he writes and records and performs, songs that often express faith in Jesus. For Myers, part of what that means is continuing to be actively involved in programs sponsored by the International Fellowship of Christians and Jews that provide practical help to Jewish emigrants to Israel. Neither man sees a conflict between faith in Jesus and support of Jewish people—who, as Myers points out, "remain the apple of God's eye, a designation which I don't believe was ever rescinded."

No one accuses Myers or his wife, Nancy, of renouncing their faith in Jesus when they actively participate in programs involving Israel and the Jewish people. Not so with Bob Dylan, though. Seemingly, every foray into the Jewish arena is interpreted as a flat-out return to Judaism, a renunciation of the truth of Jesus Christ that he confessed more than two decades ago. It seems that embracing a Judeo-Christian heritage is a privilege some would like to deny to Bob Dylan.

Overruling the wishes of some, Dylan continues to perform Christian songs, both his own compositions and his covers of gospel standards, contemporary songs, and traditional hymns. Coupled with his comments in interviews and on stage, the songs he sings indicate that the sixties icon is still very much a product and reflection of his encounter with Jesus in 1979.

Author Ronnie Keohane, a Jewish believer in Jesus, feels that both the media and the church—and no doubt, the Jewish community—have missed the boat with regard to Dylan's spiritual journey. Out of the hundreds of songs Dylan has written during his prolific career, there is only one line that Keohane believes that he could not sing as a Jewish believer in Jesus. That one line—"Even Jesus would never forgive what you do" from "Masters of War"—is the one line that Dylan has consistently omitted from his concerts since 1979. "Dylan knows it is not biblically correct, because all sins that a man can commit are possible for God to forgive," Keohane concludes.

Dylan once expressed incredulity that people considered him to be enigmatic. It's all right there in the music, he said; listen to the music, and you'll know what he thinks and believes. Yet fans and critics alike seem to have a difficult time taking him at his word when it comes to his spiritual journey. If it's really all right there in the music, then Bob Dylan is without a doubt a man who continues to express faith in Jesus while holding on to his Jewish heritage.

Dylan doesn't fit any of the religious molds that people have created, simply because Dylan's personal expression of faith remains larger than any mold mere men ever *could* create. Meanwhile, as outside observers continue their effort to pigeonhole him, Bob Dylan continues to sit at the feet of the Master on his personal hillside, listening attentively, questioning respectfully, analyzing thoughtfully.

Yes, this just could be where Dylan has been sitting all along.

NOTES

1 Scott Marshall, "A Few Words with Shirley Caesar," *On the Tracks* #20
(Winter/Spring 2001), p. 29.

2 John Bauldie, "The Wanted Man Interview: Ron Wood," *The Telegraph* #33
(Summer 1989), p. 67.

3 Dave Hoekstra, "Staples of Life and Liberty," *Chicago Sun-Times*, February 22, 2002;
http://www.suntimes.com/output/show/cst-ftr-staples22.html

4 Robert Shelton, *No Direction Home: The Life and Music of Bob Dylan*, New York:
Da Capo Press, 1997, p. 128 (originally published in 1986); Bob Dylan, "Some
Other Kinds of Songs," CD liner notes to *Another Side of Bob Dylan*, 1964, p. 4;
Stephen Pickering, *Bob Dylan Approximately: A Portrait of the Jewish Poet in Search
of God: A Midrash*, New York: David McKay Company, Inc., 1975, p. 60; Anthony
Scaduto, *Bob Dylan*, London: Helter Skelter Publishing, 1996, p. 220 (originally
published in 1971)

5 John J. Thompson, *Raised by Wolves: The Story of Christian Rock & Roll*, Toronto:
ECW Press, 2000, pp. 73-74.

6 Michael Corcoran, "Recommended: Music," *Austin American-Statesman*,
February 21, 2002.

7 Colbert S. Cartwright, "The Times They Are A-Changin': The Time-Wearied
Troubadour Turns 50," *Sojourners* (June 1991), p. 40.

8 Davin Seay and Mary Neely, *Stairway to Heaven: The Spiritual Roots of Rock and Roll*,
New York: Ballantine Books, 1986, pp. 327-328.

9 J.J. Goldberg, "Bob Dylan at 60: 'We Used to Be Young Together': A Musical Seer
Who Disdained Role of Prophet," *Forward*, May 18, 2001;
http://www.forward.com/issues/2001/01.05.18/arts4.html

10 John Herdman, *Voice Without Restraint: Bob Dylan's Lyrics and Their Background*,
New York: Delilah Books, 1982, p. 96.

11 Stephen Davis, *Old Gods Almost Dead: The 40-Year Odyssey of the Rolling Stones*,
New York: Broadway Books, 2001, p. 237.

12 Author interview, Scott Ross, 2000.

13 Bex Levine, "Let the Locusts Descend," *The Daily Princetonian*, March 12, 2001.

14 Shelton, *No Direction Home*, p. 413.

15 Neil Hickey, "A Voice Still Blowin' in the Wind," *TV Guide*, September 11, 1976.

16 Ron Rosenbaum, "Bob Dylan: A Candid Conversation With the Visionary Whose Songs Changed the Times," *Playboy*, March 1978, p. 90.

17 Sal Recchi, "The Indelible Dylan: Legend Has Left a Trail of Memories," *Orlando Sentinel*, January 25, 2002, p. 8.

18 Bert Cartwright, *The Bible in the Lyrics of Bob Dylan*, Romford, Essex, England: Wanted Man, 1992, p. 57.

19 Author interview, T-Bone Burnett, 1999.

20 Author interview, Jerry Scheff, 2001.

21 Author interview, Jenny (Yaffee) Goetz, 2001.

22 Author interview, Kleg Seth, 2001.

23 Author interview, Terry Zeyen, 2001.

24 Author interviews, Al Kasha , 1999 and 2000.

25 Author interview, Paul Wasserman, 2001.

26 Author interview, Barry Beckett, 2000.

27 Author interview, Jerry Wexler, 2000.

28 Author interview, Dick Cooper, 2000.

29 Author interview, Catherine Kanner, 2000.

30 Author interview, Nick Saxton, 2000.

31 Author interview, John Perry Barlow, 1999.

32 Author interview, Laurence Schlesinger, 2000.

33 Author interview, Philip Elwood, 1999.

34 Scott Marshall, "The On the Tracks Interview: Spooner Oldham, " *On the Tracks* #17 (Fall 1999), p. 18.

35 Author interview, Fred Tackett, 1999.

36 Author interview, Tim Drummond, 2001.

37 Author interview, Peter Barsotti, 2000.

38 Author interviews, Tim Charles, 2001.

39 Author interview, Dan Fiala, 2001.

40 "Dave Kelly Interview: Conducted by Chris Cooper, September 23, 1987,
" *Isis: A Bob Dylan Anthology*, London: Helter Skelter Publishing, 2001, p. 166.

41 "Dylan Tour Off to a Shaky Start," *Rolling Stone*, December 13, 1979.

42 Author interview, Mitch Glaser, 2001.

43 Author interview, David Whiting-Smith, 2001.

44 Bauldie (Ron Wood interview), *The Telegraph*, #33, p. 67; Janet Huck, Barbara
Oraustark, and Ying Ying Wu, "The (New) Word According to Dylan," *Newsweek*,
December 17, 1979, p. 90; Rod MacBeath, "The Bridge Interview: Bruce Gary,"
The Bridge, #8 (Winter 2000), p. 22.

45 Author interview, Leland Rucker, 2002.

46 Clinton Heylin, "Saved!: Bob Dylan's Conversion to Christianity" (Part Three),
The Telegraph #30 (Summer 1988), p. 54—except for the last four sentences of
this onstage rap which is from a transcription in an article by Patrick Webster
appearing in *Freewheelin'* Vol. 18, No. 180 (August 2000), p. 31.

47 Author interview, Peter Stone Brown, 2000.

48 Author interview, Terry Mosher ("Aislin"), 2000.

49 John Bauldie, "A Conversation with Tony Wright," *The Telegraph* #43
(Autumn 1992), p. 88, 93.

50 John Harris, "Dylan: The Guide," Q (October 2000), p. 140.

51 Author interview, Joel Selvin, 2000.

52 Author interview, Larry Sparks, 2000.

53 Michael Long, "What Good Came From the Sixties?" *The Weekly Standard*,
January 1, 2001, http://www.whwg.com/Firm/WritersSample.cfm?SampleId=31

54 Author interview, Kasriel Kastel, 2000.

55 Cooper (David Kelly interview), *Isis: A Bob Dylan Anthology*, p. 167.

56 "Has Born-Again Bob Dylan Returned to Judaism?" *Christianity Today*, January 13,
1984.

57 Bob Dylan, "Mixed Up Confusion," Copyright 1962, 1968 by Warner Bros. Inc.

58 Howard Sounes, *Down the Highway: The Life of Bob Dylan*, New York: Grove Press, 2001, p. 356.

59 Scott Marshall, "An Exclusive On the Tracks Interview: Howard Sounes," *On the Tracks* #21 (Summer 2001), p. 47.

60 "Brief Encounter: Leonard Cohen," *The Telegraph* #28 (Winter 1987), p. 94— interview conducted by unidentified journalist on March 5, 1985, in Basel, Switzerland.

61 Clinton Heylin, *Bob Dylan Behind the Shades: A Biography*, New York: Summit Books, 1991, p. 382.

62 Scott Cohen, "Don't Ask Me Nothin' About Nothin', I Might Just Tell You the Truth: Bob Dylan Revisited," *Spin*, December 1985, p. 80.

63 Ibid, p. 81.

64 Author interview, Chris Skinker, 2001.

65 Bob Spitz, *Dylan: A Biography*, New York: W.W. Norton and Company, 1991, p. 528.

66 Edna Gundersen, "The 'Oh Mercy' Interview: Part I," *On the Tracks* #3 (Spring 1994), pp. 12, 14-15—originally published in *USA Today*, September 21, 1989.

67 Sounes, *Down the Highway*, 2001, p. 390.

68 Tom Chaffin, "As Ever, Dylan Both Iconoclast and Icon," *Atlanta Journal-Constitution*, May 27, 2001, L-3.

69 Bob Dylan, "From a Man's Point of View: Adam's Rib," *Sister 2 Sister*, Vol. 2, No. 10, July 1990, p. 1, 12 (thanks to Mary McKenzie of *Sister 2 Sister* for both the fax and permission to reprint this letter).

70 Bob Dylan, lyric excerpt from "I Believe in You," Copyright 1979 by Special Rider Music.

71 Robert Hilburn, "Forever Dylan: On the Never-Ending Tour with Rock's Greatest Poet," *Los Angeles Times*, February 9, 1992 (interview conducted in November 1991).

72 Dallas Holm, lyric excerpt from "Rise Again," Copyright 1977 by Dimension Music/SESAC (all rights controlled by The Benson Company, Inc., Nashville, TN).

73 Mike Wyvill and John Wraith, "Jotting Down Notes," *The Telegraph* #46
(Summer 1993), p. 132.

74 John Dolen, "The Talk with Dylan," *On the Tracks* #7 (Spring 1996), p. 9.

75 Scott Benarde, "Rock for the Ages: Pop Stars Sing Out About Their Judaism,"
http://www.jewishjournal.com/home/searchview.php3?id=2953, August 27, 1999.

76 Larry Yudelson, "Dylan on Tour: Fall Tour 1995,"
http://www.radiohazak.com/Tours.html

77 Author interview, Chris Skinker, 2001.

78 John Thavis, "Times They Are A-Changin': Dylan to Perform for the Pope,"
Catholic Star Herald, August 29, 1997—via *Series of Dreams* #46 (1997), p. 6.

79 Mike Wyvill and John Wraith, *Take to the Road: Bob Dylan's 1997 Concerts*,
Houghton-Le-Spring: Bailes the Printer, 1998, p. 14.

80 Author interview, Ralph Stanley, 2000.

81 Richard Younger, "Dylan Takes the High Lonesome Road with Ralph Stanley:
An Exclusive On the Tracks Interview," *On the Tracks* #15 (Fall 1999), p. 34.

82 Sounes, *Down the Highway*, 2001, p. 326.

83 Ruth Rosen, *Jesus For Jews*, San Francisco: A Messianic Perspective, 1987, p.285.

84 Jon Pareles, "A Wiser Voice Blowin' in the Autumn Wind,"
New York Times, September 28, 1997.

85 Imre Salusinszky, "Chimes of Freedom Flashing: Bob Dylan's Message About
Freedom and Responsibility," *The Telegraph* #49 (Summer 1994), p. 23.

86 Author interview, Dallas Holm, 1999.

87 Alex Ross, "The Wanderer," *The New Yorker*, May 10, 1999, p. 58.

88 Author interview, Alan Jacobs, 1999.

89 Ian Woodward, "National Poetry Day and Andrew Motion," The Wicked Messenger
#4365, *Isis* #87 (October-November 1999), p. 14.

90 Larry Yudelson, "Jewish Mothers: Mum No More," *Moment* (December 1999)—
reprinted in *Series of Dreams* #71 (2000), p. 5.

91 Clinton Heylin, *Bob Dylan: Behind the Shades Revisited*, New York: William Morrow,
2001, pp. 719-720.

92 Sean Dolan, "Muddy River Country: Bob Dylan & Jerry Garcia,"
On the Tracks #7 (Spring 1996), p. 17.

93 http://www.inmusicwetrust.com (issue #30, April 2000)

94 "Jewish Top 10: The Kosher Top 10 Pop and Rock Stars,"
http://www.jewish.co.uk/top10music.php3, June 20, 2000.

95 Jan McGuinness, "Dylan's Tribe," *The Age*, March 4, 2001.

96 Steve Turner, "Watered-Down Love," *Christianity Today*, May 21, 2001, p. 90.

97 Brian Doherty, "The Free-Floating Bob Dylan," *Reason*, November 2001, p. 55
(thanks to Professor John Lawing, the legendary cartoonist).

98 Edna Gundersen, "Forever Dylan," *USA Today*, May 18, 2001, 2E.

99 David Vest, "Whose Bob Dylan?" (*http://www.mindspring.com/~dcqv/dylan.htm*).

100 Goldberg, "Bob Dylan at 60: 'We Used to Be Young Together'"
(http://www.forward.com/issues/2001/01.05.18/arts4.html).

101 "Carolyn Dennis," *Follow Your Dream International* (December 1992); an excerpt
from a Bruce Springsteen fanzine posted on the Internet
(*http://www.interferenza.com/bcs/articles/carol.htm*).

102 "Newspapermen Eating Candy: The Rome Press Conference," *Isis* #99
(October-November 2001), pp. 47-48, 50.

103 Robert Hilburn, "How Does It Feel?: Don't Ask," *Los Angeles Times*,
September 16, 2001.

104 Mikal Gilmore, "The Rolling Stone Interview: Bob Dylan," *Rolling Stone*,
November 22, 2001, pp. 56-69.

105 Hoekstra, "Staples of Life and Liberty," February 22, 2002
(http://www.suntimes.com/output/show/cst-ftr-staples22.html).

106 Bob Dylan, "Solid Rock," Copyright 1980 by Special Rider Music.

107 Author interview, Larry Myers, 1999.

108 Sounes, *Down the Highway*, 2001, p. 331.

109 Author interview, Regina Havis, 1999.

ALSO FROM RELEVANT BOOKS

THE GOSPEL ACCORDING TO TONY SOPRANO

THE GOSPEL ACCORDING TO TONY SOPRANO reveals that *The Sopranos* is much like a biblical parable. It provokes us, challenges us, and pries back the exterior to peek into the darkest parts of our souls. This book explores the many reasons why the show has connected so deeply with American culture and exposes the mysteries of life and faith that emerges just behind the curtains of baked ziti and Armani suits.

I AM RELEVANT

Profiles a wide range of people ages 18-34 who in some way break the walls of tradition in fulfilling the Great Commission. Each story is a statement of faith and a testimony of grace. These people are making a difference, and this book shares their stories. In its pages, you'll find inspiration to make your own.

GOD WHISPERS: Learning To Hear His Voice

We have questions. God has answers. We just don't always hear them. GOD WHISPERS challenges readers to live with a tender heart as well as open eyes and ears to the countless ways in which God speaks.

IF YOU LIKE THIS BOOK, YOU'LL LOVE
RELEVANTMAGAZINE.COM

RELEVANTMAGAZINE.COM is an out of-the-box publication covering God, life and progressive culture like nothing else. Updated with new content daily, the site discusses faith, career, relationships, music and more from an intelligent, God-centered perspective. In style, substance and focus, there's nothing like RELEVANTMAGAZINE.COM.

FEATURING:

[-] Articles, columns, news and reviews updated daily

[-] Message boards and chat

[-] Weekly newsletter

[-] Free downloads

[-] Online store with a ton of RELEVANT gear and books

[-] Want to be updated on hot new features and news from RELEVANT? Sign up for our weekly email, 850 WORDS OF RELEVANT. It's the best email you'll receive all week.